# Diversity, Equity, Accessibility, and Inclusion in Museums

## AMERICAN ALLIANCE OF MUSEUMS

The American Alliance of Museums has been bringing museums together since 1906, helping to develop standards and best practices, gathering and sharing knowledge, and providing advocacy on issues of concern to the entire museum community. Representing more than thirty-five thousand individual museum professionals and volunteers, institutions, and corporate partners serving the museum field, the alliance stands for the broad scope of the museum community.

The American Alliance of Museums' mission is to champion museums and nurture excellence in partnership with its members and allies.

Books published by AAM further the Alliance's mission to make standards and best practices for the broad museum community widely available.

 American Alliance of Museums

# Diversity, Equity, Accessibility, and Inclusion in Museums

Edited by
Johnnetta Betsch Cole and Laura L. Lott

ROWMAN & LITTLEFIELD
*Lanham • Boulder • New York • London*

Published by Rowman & Littlefield
A wholly owned subsidary of The Rowman & Littlefield Publishing Group, Inc.
4501 Forbes Boulevard, Suite 200, Lanham, Maryland 20706
www.rowman.com

6 Tinworth Street, London SE11 5AL, United Kingdom

British Library Cataloguing in Publication Information Available

**Library of Congress Cataloging-in-Publication Data**

Names: Cole, Johnnetta B., editor. | Lott, Laura L., editor.
Title: Diversity, equity, accessibility, and inclusion in museums / edited by
  Johnnetta Betsch Cole and Laura L. Lott.
Description: Lanham : Rowman & Littlefield Publishers, [2019] | Series:
  American Alliance of Museums | Includes bibliographical references and
  index.
Identifiers: LCCN 2018046109 (print) | LCCN 2018056403 (ebook) | ISBN
  9781538118641 (Electronic) | ISBN 9781538118634 (cloth : alk. paper) |
  ISBN 9781538118627 (pbk. : alk. paper)
Subjects: LCSH: Museums and minorities—United States. | Museums—Social
  aspects—United States. | Museum visitors—United States. | Social
  integration—United States.
Classification: LCC AM11 (ebook) | LCC AM11 .D625 2019 (print) | DDC
  069/.108—dc23
LC record available at https://lccn.loc.gov/2018046109

♾™ The paper used in this publication meets the minimum requirements of American
National Standard for Information Sciences—Permanence of Paper for Printed Library
Materials, ANSI/NISO Z39.48-1992.

Printed in the United States of America

## DEDICATION

James D. Staton, Jr.     Steven E. Lott

These are the     wonderful men,
our loving partners, to whom we
dedicate this volume—for their
support & understanding that
it's not about who stands
behind whom, but
about standing
together.

—JBC
LLL

# Contents

# Preface

Diversity, equity, accessibility, and inclusion (DEAI), in all aspects of museums' structures and programming, are issues of vital importance to the museum field. These principles are the foundation of public museums' values—morally and ethically—and they are also the foundation for museums to remain relevant to an increasingly diverse population. Much has been written and discussed about the imperatives, the challenges, and the inadequate progress we have made as a field. Yet these important essays, conference sessions, research reports, and blog posts are scattered about and, too often, lost.

This edited volume is a collection of many of the most important essays, presentations, and reports on these topics from the past several decades—from Lonnie Bunch's seminal article, "Flies in the Buttermilk: Museums, Diversity, and the Will to Change," first published in 2000, to Johnnetta Betsch Cole's keynote speech at the 2015 American Alliance of Museums' Annual Meeting, to new writings, data, and analysis from emerging leaders in the push for greater equity. The works in this volume include calls to action, strategies for embedding DEAI in museum strategy and process, and stories of personal journeys toward greater equity in museums. While it is impossible to capture the full diversity of the world's people, we have represented much of it in who the authors are and their diverse perspectives.

This volume is not a how-to guide for greater inclusion in museums. Rather, it seeks to facilitate a much-needed intergenerational dialogue that helps build on lessons from the past, broadens our thinking about the many different facets of this complex work we abbreviate simply as DEAI, and ignites inspiration for continuing—indeed accelerating—this work across museums of all types, sizes, and locations.

Here are three among the important questions posed in this collection of writings:

- Why do challenges of inequity and inaccessibility in museums persist?
- How will a new generation of museum leaders change this picture—to better represent the communities museums strive to engage and serve?

- What can we learn from those who have been observing, experiencing, and writing about these issues?

This book is designed for a wide variety of readers and audiences. We hope this text will be required reading for all who are studying, working in, and governing museums.

Together, we can and we must make diversity, equity, accessibility, and inclusion central to museology and excellent museum practice.

# Acknowledgments

This book presents the work of many contributors whose thought leadership and dedication to the work of diversity, equity, accessibility, and inclusion (DEAI) in the cultural sector and beyond inspires us each day. We are extremely grateful to those who penned essays for this volume and those who granted permission for us to include their previously published essays and remarks as guideposts along the field's journey toward greater equity.

There are also many others whose thought leadership and hard work have influenced ours, including our colleagues on the board and staff of the American Alliance of Museums (AAM), the Association of Art Museum Directors (AAMD), the Andrew W. Mellon Foundation, the Ford Foundation, the Walton Family Foundation, and Cook Ross, Inc.

We acknowledge the members of the AAM Working Group on Diversity, Equity, Accessibility, and Inclusion, which we were honored to co-chair last year with leadership from Kathy Dwyer Southern, Brooke Leonard, and Nicole Ivy. The working group conversations over nine months inspired and prompted us to publish this book. We are profoundly grateful to each member of the working group for their probing questions, thoughtful ideas and insights, and their very special friendships.

Our executive editor, Charles Harmon, encouraged and nurtured our concept for this book from the very beginning. We thank Charles and his colleagues at Rowman & Littlefield for their guidance and support in publishing this book, as well as our indexer, Jennifer Rushing-Schurr of White Oak Indexing.

This project would simply not have been possible without our talented research assistant, Frances M. Grant, who contributed countless hours, edits, and ideas that made this book what it is. Committed to examining the intersections between art and society, Frances aspires to be an art writer and curator.

# Part 1

## A CALL TO ACTION

# 1

## Flies in the Buttermilk

### Museums, Diversity, and the Will to Change

*Lonnie G. Bunch III*

*This essay was originally published in the July/August 2000 issue of* Museum News, *published by the American Alliance of Museums.*

When I first attended national meetings of the museum professionals in the late 1970s, I was struck by how few people of color were present. I remember searching the crowd for the nod of recognition or the acknowledgment and acceptance that comes from a common cultural connection. I knew we would find each other eventually, share effusive greetings, and joke once again about the "joys" of integrating the profession. In a corner of the convention center, or in the rear of the vendors' marketplace, we would prepare ourselves for the sessions by singing the words of Al Green's 1971 hit, "I'm so tired of being alone, I'm so tired of being on my own." Invariably after attending a session, we would reconvene and someone, drawing on his knowledge of southern folklore, would say "There were just a few of us flies in the buttermilk." Reminding us, though we needed no reminder, that the museum field was awash in whiteness.

When I entered the main hall of the Baltimore Convention Center during the AAM Annual Meeting this May [2000], I was pleased to see a greater sprinkling of diverse attendees. No longer were the numbers so small that we seemed almost invisible. Yet even that pleasure was tempered by the fact that many of the people of color who attended the gathering represented ethnic or racially specific institutions. While it is crucial that the professional organizations service a more diverse institutional base, the mere presence of more African Americans, Asian Americans, Latinos, or Native peoples at annual meetings does not mean that museums that once called themselves "mainstream" have wrestled effectively and creatively with issues of diversity and staffing. In fact, a visit to almost any museum leaves one startled by just how small the numbers really are. The limited minority presence in the professional ranks of America's cultural institutions is a sad comment on the museum profession's inability to create a permanent workforce that reflects the diversity of this nation. It dramatically reveals the great chasm between the profession's stated ideals and its daily practices and priorities.

No one can deny that the profession espouses the need to explore the issue of diversity. In the past decade, it has been impossible to attend a meeting that has not had a session or a paper that looks at some aspect of cultural diversity. For example, the AAM meeting in Baltimore had twelve sessions that were included in a "Diversity Pathway" and more than thirty panels that examined some aspect of "multiculturalism." Almost all the recently drafted mission statements of museums promise a greater appreciation of America's heterogeneity. And publications like *Excellence and Equity: Education and the Public Dimension of Museums* (AAM, 1992) encourage the profession to embrace diversity. According to *Excellence and Equity*:

> If museums are to be welcoming places for people of different racial, ethnic, social, economic, and educational backgrounds, and if they are to use their collections to present a variety of perspectives, they must recruit, hire or select, and foster the professional growth of trustees, staff, and volunteers who reflect diverse audiences and multiple perspectives.

Clearly the rhetoric of change and diversity has echoed throughout the museum profession. And if rhetoric alone could effect change, then our profession would stand transformed. Unfortunately, words are not enough.

Despite more than a decade of conversation, we have failed to address adequately, seriously, and creatively the realities of a less than diverse workforce. In a recent national survey that assessed the financial situation of America's museums (*1999 AAM Museum Financial Information: A Report from the National Survey*), one question asked the ethnic or racial background of the top institutional administrator. Only 4.2 percent of museum directors were people of color. Of that percentage, 1 percent were African American, 1.2 percent were American Indian, 0.5 percent were Asian American, 0.2 percent were Pacific Islanders, and 1.3 percent Latino. I suspect that the numbers would be much lower if the directors of ethnic or racially specific institutions were eliminated from this survey. A total of less than 2 percent would not be surprising. It is hard to understand why a profession so seemingly committed to diversity would have such a difficult time creating a more varied cadre of leaders.

The problem, however, is not only at the top. Several years ago, I discovered that many of the lower-level curatorial staff at the National Museum of American History who were African American were retiring early to take advantage of a government buyout program. Most of these employees had worked at the Smithsonian Institution for more than thirty years. During a farewell luncheon, they reminded me that except for their mass hiring in the 1960s, the museum had failed to bring mid- and entry-level African Americans into the museum. Though they applauded the recent appointment of several minority curators, they startled me by saying that once "we leave, the professional staff at the museum will be whiter than it was in 1963." And it is not clear that the future, if we hold to the current attitudes and practices, will be much better. An examination of the nation's premiere programs in museum studies and museum education reveals a minority presence that is so low it is embarrassing. Few programs have more than one or two students of color. Several are without any. Other programs have as many as nine or ten students but the numbers fluctuate wildly on an annual basis. Clearly the profession has reached a crossroad. Do we continue to muddle along, or do we find the creativity, the resources, and most important, the will to change?

Finding the will is crucial. In recent years the museum profession has wrestled successfully with several complex and difficult issues, from the repatriation of Native American human remains and cultural objects to Nazi loot to broader international concerns about the illegal appropriation of cultural patrimony. This success stems in part from a clear recognition and definition of the problem, which helped galvanize the profession and challenge cultural institutions to focus scarce but much needed intellectual, financial, and emotional resources on these concerns. This sense of urgency, this accumulation of resources and will, is impressive. But it leads me to wonder why this is not the case when it comes to creating a more culturally diverse staff. Why is there a lack of will that is inconsistent with the manner in which the profession usually faces a crisis? What is it that makes progress in this area so incremental and so glacial? And more important, what should museums do now to create a more meaningfully diverse profession? In order to further this discussion, I would like to suggest some ideas and possible future directions that may help us accelerate the pace of change.

Not too long ago, I was leaning against the wall by the staff elevators at the National Museum of American History, daydreaming. Suddenly a woman who was clearly in a hurry and clearly very blond rushed up to me and demanded that I "quickly get the elevator because she was late for a meeting" with senior management of the museum. At first I was so startled that I could barely utter an almost unintelligible "What?" Showing her frustration, she said, "I was told that an elevator operator would take me to the fifth floor, so take me there." Realizing that she mistook me for the elevator operator, I became so angry that I was speechless. At that moment the elevator door opened and a museum guard greeted me by asking, "How's life, Mister Associate Director?" Discerning that she had made a mistake, the woman began an apology by saying "Sorry, I just assumed . . ."

"I just assumed. . . ." These unspoken assumptions often blind us to the possible. They can muddy and interfere with our best efforts. And they make it difficult to see the extent and the depth of a problem. In essence, many of the obstacles that limit the profession's ability to improve its record on developing and maintaining a more varied workforce stem from incorrect assumptions, unrealistic expectations, and imprecise definitions. Why, for example, do many in the field assume that a gathering of museum directors—all of whom are white—is an acceptable occurrence? Or why did many Americans share Tavis Smiley's on-air shock (Smiley is a commentator for black television and radio programs) when he learned that Lisa Stevens, the curator at the National Zoo responsible for the care of the pandas, is African American?

Smiley just assumed that "no one in a position of authority at the Smithsonian was black." It is essential that as a profession we reassess and reevaluate some of our basic assumptions and help the public do the same.

One assumption that hinders our efforts at change involves the reasons for the perceived scarcity of people of color who are willing to enter either our training programs or labor in our cultural institutions. A museum director of a large southern historical society recently shared his frustrations at not being able to hire an African American museum educator because "it seems that many [people of color] with advanced training can make more money in other fields." The chair of a museum studies program in the Northeast bemoaned his program's failure to lure minority students to campus. "The museum field does not pay well and they tend to head toward higher-paying jobs." It is true that many college-trained minorities seek the financial rewards of business or management careers. But so do most white college graduates.

It is a fallacy that there are not significant numbers of African Americans, Latinos, American Indians, and Asian Americans who care passionately about art, history, and science, and who would work, gladly, in cultural institutions that valued diversity, nurtured staff, and offered challenging careers. These arguments remind me of discussions that the profession had in the 1980s about why museums were facing resistance to their well-intentioned community outreach programs. Many in the field wondered "why these community groups do not appreciate the importance of history or were unwilling to share their culture" with museums. Today, we know differently. The real issue is not money but the monochromatic nature of our institutions. If we are to entice the best and the brightest to our field, regardless of race, then we must change our strategies, our culture, and our assumptions.

Another assumption that limits our effectiveness is how we define and address diversity. Carl Sandburg once wrote of Chicago that it was "a city of broad shoulders." In some ways, the museum field treats diversity as if it were "a city of broad shoulders," capable of encompassing almost any aspect of museum life. So much of what we do is viewed as falling under the shadow of diversity. Whenever museums create a new community outreach endeavor, this is seen as another successful diversity initiative. When a new museum-school partnership is announced, it is viewed as another notable example of how the profession is grappling with diversity. While it is true that many of these collaborations are important indicators of change, we are still not addressing the central problem. These successes often deflect our attention and our resources from the core issue: diversifying the permanent staff of America's museums. Until we change the tint and tone of our workforce, we are just dancing around the edges of our greatest failure. After all, a heterogeneous staff is the engine that makes all the other "diversity" endeavors possible. Museums all seek to develop long-term, mutually reciprocal relationships with a dizzying array of communities. Yet why should these groups really believe our rhetoric of cultural transformation unless we are willing to exert the energy and make the hard choices that accompany the creation of a meaningfully diverse profession? We champion the practice of community outreach. But I think we need to promote "inreach," a concept that challenges the profession to be more introspective, more deliberate, more honest, and more explicit in its efforts to change itself.

In his novel *The Fire Next Time*, James Baldwin wrote "Americans are a people trapped by traditions, traditions so strong that their origins are forgotten but they still carry great weight." So what can museums do to break the traditions and challenge the assumptions that weigh us down, that impede change? What concrete steps would help the profession's diversity? First, the field must accept the fact that despite all of its publicized efforts to embrace diversity, changing the face of the profession has met with limited success. And that this lack of success is a legitimate threat to much of what museums claim as their agenda for the twenty-first century. It is time that the issue of staff diversity move to the top of the priority list for all our museums. It is wonderful that people of color are now represented on the councils and advisory boards of the professional organizations. Yet without a more diverse presence in all aspects of a museum's hierarchy and structure, even these important changes seem more cosmetic than substantive.

The museum field also must realize that the problems of diversity confronting our institutions are too significant and so complex that the solutions lie in a collaborative and concerted effort that transcends the piecemeal and ad hoc approaches of the past. Addressing these issues in a meaningful manner is far too great a task for a single museum, a section of the profession, or for the lone foundation or university. What the field needs is a comprehensive scheme that leverages resources, builds upon proven successes, and fosters collaboration and communication among professional organizations, funding sources, and universities. I think there is a need for a summit, a gathering of the best minds, for a pan-profession, interdisciplinary examination of the challenges of diversity that confront American museums. This conclave of scholars, museum leaders, educators, politicians, trustees, foundation officers, and community representatives would do more than simply sound the alarm. It would be tasked to develop concrete plans and publications, determine model programs, outline possible financial support, create strategies to garner political and media support, and, ultimately, generate a blueprint for successful change. This blueprint must be as all-encompassing and as creative as the Marshall Plan, the post–World War II effort to reshape and rebuild Europe. Diversifying the profession will take intellectual, financial, and political resourcefulness and commitment.

Sometimes, committing to change requires prodding. Two areas that have traditionally influenced museum policy have been accreditation and funding agencies. I would suggest that our institutions would change more quickly if the development of a more diverse staff were one of the elements that contributed to the granting of accreditation. Since its inception, the accreditation process has been used to elevate the level of professionalism and expertise throughout the field. In recent years, accreditation has encouraged the profession to embrace long-range planning, more sophisticated interpretive programming, and the need to expand our public dimension. If diversifying the professional staff is truly one of the stated priorities of the field, then it is quite appropriate that achieving accreditation be tied to that goal. After all, is not the role of the accreditation process to help establish and promote the higher standards to which museums should aspire? By declaring that a diverse staff will now be a standard for excellence, this issue may finally get the attention and action it deserves.

During my youth, our neighborhood gas station had a sign above the cash register that read "cash makes no enemies, let's be friends." Clearly the museum profession spends a great deal of time looking for friends with cash. These friends, especially those who work for foundations, have the opportunity to help the profession achieve a more heterogeneous workforce. Many foundations have generously supported museum activities involving diversity. It would be interesting if more foundations collaborated and pooled their resources to better leverage their impact, such as the Ford Foundation and Philip Morris fellowships that support underrepresented artists. More interesting still would be if foundations began to use staff diversity as one of their granting criteria. In some ways, this would have a great impact on the field, similar to the manner in which the National Endowment for the Humanities' insistence upon rigorous scholarship has reshaped the interpretive presentations in history museums.

Another realm that dramatically affects the field's ability to diversify is the area of training and education. Many in the profession claim that the lack of "trained and qualified" people of color is the major factor why museums are less than diverse. Yet there are model programs that have impressive results in shaping and supporting minorities who are interested in joining the profession. One of the most successful endeavors is the Atlanta History Center/Coca-Cola Foundation (now National) Museum Fellows Program, established in 1994. This wonderful undertaking is dedicated to developing strong minority students who will eventually work in the museum field. This kind of program deserves the profession's support so that it can be emulated throughout the nation. And there are other thriving endeavors, such as the College Art Association's Development Fellowship Program, that can be effective models to help the profession's diversity. What is missing is the comprehensive strategy that will enable the field to discover, acknowledge, support, and build upon this important work.

I confess, I am worried. Worried because after more than twenty years in this field, I am still hearing some of the same debates and conversations. Worried because I cannot fully answer the question of why, with so many people of talent and color in this country, more of them are not running our major institutions, leading our curatorial departments, and shaping our educational agendas. Worried because after two decades, I am still "so tired of being alone."

Clearly, there is much to do. The museum field, the profession I love, has to make the commitment to change. It is not a choice, it is an obligation. And it should not be an onerous obligation. We should live up to our stated ideals. If we truly believe that we are a better profession when we embrace diversity, then let that diversity permeate and shape the staff throughout our museums, galleries, science centers, and zoos. It is in our power to change this profession—if we have the courage, the creativity, and the will.

# 2

# Museums, Racism, and the Inclusiveness Chasm

*Carlos Tortolero*

*This essay was originally published in the November/December 2000 issue of* Museum News, *published by the American Alliance of Museums.*

The article by Lonnie Bunch, "Museums, Diversity, and the Will to Change" (July/ August 2000), reminded me how far we still have to go. The article was well written and informative, but the author failed to get to the heart of the matter.

There are hundreds of thousands of people of color with college degrees and thousands who are qualified to serve on boards, yet the number of people of color at the so-called mainstream museums is still relatively low. If you gave any statistician such information, how would he or she account for it? Considering all the numbers, the statistician would likely conclude that racism is one of the main reasons there are so few people of color in the museum field.

I have attended dozens of panels through the years at which museum personnel supposedly talk about diversity, but the presenters are always dodging the real issue. In his article, Bunch provides excellent clear-cut examples of racism, yet he never invokes the term. The museum field, like society at large, has a problem with racism and must face up to it. First, we in museums, like the rest of society, need to admit that we have a problem. Then and only then can we move forward.

Before I discuss museums and diversity further, let me give you my background. I am the founder and executive director of the Mexican Fine Arts Center Museum in Chicago, the largest Latino arts organization in the country, and the only Latino museum accredited by the American Association of Museums (now the American Alliance of Museums). I am a firm believer in the concept of "First Voice" and the special perspective brought to the museum field by institutions such as the Studio Museum in Harlem, el Museo del Barrio, and the Mexican Fine Arts Center Museum. Yet I also strongly believe that the cultures of people of color must be represented at the large museums throughout the country.

There's a lot of hypocrisy in the museum field and arts world. We attack the Right for censoring the NEA, yet we are guilty of wordsmithing or, rather, double speak when we tackle uncomfortable issues that pertain to how the museum field conducts itself. Even the use of the word *diversity* is part of the problem. What we are really talking about is integrating mainstream institutions. We should use diversity as a complement, not as a replacement, to integration. But, like the word *racism*, integration is often for too many people a reminder of the turbulent '60s. We want to sugarcoat these terms to make them more palatable and make ourselves feel less threatened by the crucial issues facing our museums and society at large.

To deal successfully with integration, we have to deal with the most powerful reason why, in the twenty-first century, we are still struggling with issues of fairness and equality. That reason is racism. A friend of mine in the arts field says she dislikes talking about diversity with me because I always make her feel uneasy. I tell her that the next time I talk about diversity and racism, I'll bring her some balloons and candy. The museum field needs to stop pussyfooting around its failure to be inclusive and deal with it once and for all.

Too many people in our society and in museums see integration as a challenge that society has successfully met. They see racism as something that happened years ago in the South, when racists like George Wallace stood on a university's steps denying African Americans the right to attend. But they don't want to understand that allowing only a few people of color to become museum directors or hold high-level museum positions is just as racist.

Whenever I bring up the lack of inclusiveness in the museum world in meetings, people start moving in their seats or develop a "here-we-go-again" expression on their faces. I would wager most European Americans working at mainstream museums would say that the glass is half full or more than half full. It's not about whether the glass is half full or half empty. I would say that the glass holds barely any water at all. We don't have an inclusiveness divide; we have an inclusiveness chasm.

By now some of you reading this article are saying to yourselves that people like me should be happy with all the progress on diversity the museum field has made, and that people like me, who simply have an axe to grind, just can't be pleased. Such opinions are some of the greatest obstacles to achieving true equity in museums. Yes, things are better than they were thirty years ago, or twenty years ago, or even ten years ago. But many people of color who work in the museum field would agree with me that in the past five years museums have begun paralleling our society and acting as though they have solved the institutional racism issue.

In defense of mainstream museums (I try to be fair), one thing I have learned about integrating these institutions is that many people who work at them honestly don't get it. Some of them can probably remember a time when there weren't any people of color on their boards or on their staffs, in any professional capacity, and they believe that diversity has been achieved. I remember a prominent national art museum director arguing with me that if there were one hundred people in a room and, among them, one person of color, then that room would be diverse! This director is really a marvelous and kind person, but just doesn't get it when it comes to diversity. This ignorance—not knowing—is really a key obstacle in motivating museums to reflect the demographics in this country. Let's face it, the majority of European Americans in this country don't live in a diverse society, but they think they do. Most people of color live in two worlds—our own cultural world and the mainstream world. Consequently, serious and sincere efforts by mainstream museums to integrate sometimes fail because the people running these institutions don't have the knowledge, expertise, staffs, boards, or contacts to diversify their institutions.

Another barrier to integrating museums is that many directors eager to make the necessary changes in their institutions find their hands tied by their boards. Or the trustees are reluctant to make the widespread changes that are often needed to integrate their institutions appropriately.

As a sports fan, I can cite many examples of a new coach coming to a team and in a very short period of time turning the team completely around. So why can't museums do the same? Dick Vermeil, the former coach of the St. Louis Rams, took over a truly atrocious football team and in three years won the Super Bowl. How did he do it? It's simple. He had a mandate to do whatever it took to make his team win. Furthermore, he wasn't afraid of making comprehensive changes to accomplish this goal. If people weren't part of his program, they were let go. When it comes to being inclusive of all people, when will museums be given a mandate to be inclusive?

It always amazes me how many diversity workshops are run by white diversity consultants. Even when people of color, because they live in two worlds, are better equipped to deal with the issue of integration, they are unable to get the jobs. But to be honest, I don't believe in diversity workshops. If I were hired to do a museum workshop on diversity, all I would say is the following: God as the First Artist created a world where diversity is everywhere. Then God in his or her wisdom created a diverse group of people, who are different, but are equal. I would then tell the participants that any museum staff member or trustee who doesn't make integration a super-important priority at his or her institution should leave the museum field. It's that simple. We're not dealing with nuclear physics here.

Let's face it, museums are very conservative institutions and are reluctant and afraid to take on the issue of the "culture" of mainstream museums. Many of these institutions were created for the elite and never saw themselves as serving society as a whole. Now museums are reacting to the pressure to change. Unfortunately, this pressure usually comes from outside, rather than inside, the institution, especially where funding sources are concerned. Many mainstream institutions have placed the issue of inclusiveness on the back burner.

The 1992 AAM report, *Excellence and Equity: Education and the Public Dimension of Museums*, is a perfect example of how the mainstream museums don't get it. *Excellence and Equity* is typical of the white paper (please, no pun intended) that the mainstream produces to try to address a serious issue. It has a clever and catchy title. It makes a few points that for the museum field are, oh my gosh, a bit strong. It then becomes the Bible until the next study comes along and the cycle continues. As I tell colleagues, if *Excellence and Equity* is your Bible when it comes to being inclusive, my advice is to change your religion!

One thing that always makes me sick to my stomach is whenever I hear someone in a mainstream institution say that he or she would love to hire more people of color but can't find them. Give me a break! Where in the world are you looking? Are people of color playing hide and seek? As the executive director of a museum, I have hired many Mexican professionals. Why is it that I can find Mexicans, but the mainstream museums can't? Am I smarter than they are? Do I have better eyesight than they do? The idea that there are no qualified candidates of color is ludicrous. I have known many museum professionals of color with the "right" credentials who have been bypassed for jobs. Furthermore, there has been a trend in recent years in the museum field to hire nonmuseum professionals in such areas as education, public relations, marketing, and even for the museum director's job. Yet mainstream museums are still unable to find people of color.

Part of the problem with changing the racial and ethnic composition of museums lies with some of the people of color who work at these institutions. They need to speak up and educate their institutions about being inclusive. Too often they believe that since they have museum jobs, their communities have "made it" and that there is no problem, at least at their institutions. As executive director of a culturally grounded museum, I believe it is imperative that individuals like me have serious dialogues with other mainstream cultural institutions and museums. To that end, the Mexican Fine Arts Center Museum has probably done as many collaborations with mainstream museums and cultural institutions as any museum in the country. Most of the time, it isn't easy. But if I see progress, no matter how small, I feel good that things are moving in the right direction. However, I also have turned down or dropped out of collaborations that I felt were more about accommodating funders or trustees than about trying to make change at the institution.

You know, I love my job, I have the best job in the world. I have the pleasure and honor of sharing my culture with both my community and the larger community as well. I never want to leave my institution. But if I had another life, I would cherish the challenge of integrating a mainstream museum because I know that it can be done. I have no doubt. However, it would mean getting rid of people who aren't on the same page.

It really scares me to see the continual unwillingness of mainstream museums to treat people with equity. If museums cannot deal with diverse groups, then one has to assume that the country can't either. What does that mean for our nation's future?

# 3

# Museums, Diversity, and Social Value

*Johnnetta Betsch Cole*

*This essay was adapted from remarks delivered at the 2015 AAM Annual Meeting.*

What I have chosen to do in this keynote address is to make the case that our museums can and must be of social value by not only inspiring but creating change around one of the most critical issues of our time—the issue of diversity. That means inspiring and creating far greater diversity in our workforces, our exhibitions, our educational programs, and among our visitors.

I want to turn to our colleagues who are here from museums around the world to say this: as I discuss the need for greater diversity in U.S. museums, please know that I know that your realities may be quite different in terms of diversity. I only hope that some of the points I will make will be helpful to you.

I also want to acknowledge that I am drawing most heavily on the question of diversity in art museums given my experience and expertise in the area. To my colleagues who work in zoological parks and aquariums, while I know that you too are wrestling with questions of diversity, I humbly acknowledge my lack of expertise in the application of the principles of diversity to your unique settings. Therefore, while I may not mention or make specific references to your institutions, I trust you are able to take the principles outlined herein and apply them naturally and rigorously to your own institutions.

Colleagues, I believe that we can neither fully carry out the visions and the missions of our museums, nor can our museums continue to be of social value, if we do not do what is required to have more diversity in who works in our museums, in the work we present in our museums, in the audiences we welcome to our museums, and in the philanthropic and board leadership in our museums.

One of my "sheroes," the late Dr. Maya Angelou, issued a call to all women and men who are parents when she said: "It is time for parents to teach young people early on that in diversity there is beauty and there is strength." In our museums, we have the possibility to teach that same important message.

When we look back at the history of American museums, we see that they were products of and reflections of the political, economic, and social times. Back in the day, museums were run by and largely catered to middle-aged, middle-income, and upper-class White folks. And the collections, exhibitions, and educational programs reflected what one of my colleagues, Dr. Beverly Guy-Sheftall at Spelman College, calls the Three W's: Western places and ideas, the tastes of White folk (who were the majority of staff and visitors), and Womanless exhibitions (in that women were treated as an object of art, seen through the male gaze, not as creators of art).

Let me briefly reference my own experience with museums "back in the day." Like all African Americans who grew up in the pre–civil rights days of legal segregation in the South, as a youngster I went to colored schools, used the colored "public" library, only drank from colored water fountains, and could only sit in the back of the bus. There were no art galleries or museums where I or any Black people could visit. But how fortunate I was to have a mother who had a passion for visual arts. As we say in the art world, "She had the eye!" And she had the will and the means to adorn our home with reproductions of artworks that ironically, I would not have seen in museums had I been permitted to visit them. For in our home were reproductions of masterworks of African American artists, and books on the art of Henry Tanner, Romare Bearden, Elizabeth Catlett, Jacob Lawrence, Lois Mailou Jones, Charles White, Augusta Savage, and Aaron Douglas.

Today, with legalized segregation being a thing of the past, I can go to any museum whose entrance fee—if there is one—I can afford. And yet, too often I will not find much in those museums that reflects the history, "herstory," culture, and art of who I am, or of underrepresented people of our country and the world.

Today, from a legal standpoint, every American museum must honor EEO guidelines. Beyond compliance, there is a moral rectitude and creative benefit to having diversity in our museums' staff, boards, programs, and audiences. It is also the smart thing to do if we want our museums to be vibrant twenty-first-century places that reflect the diversity of our nation and the world.

A comprehensive look at diversity in our museums would include an assessment of the presence and the absence of the range of underrepresented groups. That is people whose primary identity is based on their race, ethnicity, gender, sexual orientation, age, religion, nationality, class, or physical abilities and disabilities. I have used the term "primary identity" because each of us has multiple identities, and it is quite possible for someone to belong to more than one of these groups. Audre Lorde had a wonderful way of making this point about our multiple identities. I had the privilege and the joy of knowing and learning from Audre Lorde when we both taught at Hunter College. Before she would begin a talk and offer a reading from her work, she would introduce herself by saying: "I am Audre Lorde, a Black, woman, feminist, lesbian, professor, poet, mother, warrior!" And then she would say, "Please do not relate to me as if I have but one identity. For I do not wake up in the morning and from 7 a.m. to 8 a.m. I am Black. But when 8 a.m. comes I become a woman, and only for an hour because at 9 a.m. I will be a feminist, only to become a lesbian on the stroke of 10 a.m."

Embracing, encouraging, and sustaining a diverse workforce in our museums is the right thing to do, because there should be an equal opportunity for all qualified people to not only enter the workforce at our museums, but to be welcomed there and supported to advance there. It is also the smart thing to do. There is a business case for diversity. If businesses are to compete effectively in this global economy, they must have within their company employees of diverse backgrounds who will bring different and innovative ideas to the table. It is also my experience that being with people of diverse backgrounds can be and often is intellectually exciting. The intellectual stimulation spurs greater creativity and innovation, both for artists and administrators.

This business case for diversity in American companies, and in our museums, rests heavily on demographic realities. Over the past few decades there have been massive demographic and social shifts. According to U.S. Census data, currently 35 percent of all U.S. residents are "minorities." Demographers have stated that this trend will not only continue but will accelerate well into the next several decades. In the next thirty years, the United States will become a majority-minority country with White folks no longer in the majority.

The future of American philanthropy, like the future of everything else in the country, will be shaped by increasing racial and ethnic diversity. According to the Minnesota Council on Foundations, "Who donates and what they give will be profoundly impacted, and public policy will become more representative of minority communities."

As Arnold Lehman, the former director of the Brooklyn Museum, puts it: "For our museums, diversity is a 'critical issue'" and "the most important book any museum director should read is the U.S. Census."

What is the state of workforce diversity in our American museums? Today, the professional staff at most American museums do not mirror the diversity of American people. Currently 20 percent of art museum staff in all positions are people of color, with the overwhelming majority working in security and maintenance positions. In the 241 museums of the Association of Art Museum Directors (AAMD), fewer than 5 percent have people of color in senior management positions.

Tony Hirschel, former director of the Smart Museum of Art at the University of Chicago, who led an AAMD task force on diversifying membership, has said this: "Few museums would say that their staffs are as diverse as they should be." Which begs the question that he has implicitly asked: "How can we create a new stream of professionals that is more diverse?"

Of course, once a museum is successful in recruiting a diverse staff, the question is: what kind of environment, atmosphere, and culture will these diverse colleagues encounter? I cannot stress enough the importance of an inclusive culture that says in countless ways: "All colleagues from all backgrounds are welcome at this museum table!"

In addition to asking about racial and ethnic diversity among museum staff, we must also ask who visits our museums? While people of color make up over one-third of the American population, according to a National Endowment for the Arts report, they make up only 9 percent of museum visitors.

As Ford Bell, President of the American Alliance of Museums, has said, "The big challenge is going to be how museums deal with the increasingly diverse American public, which could be 30 percent or more Hispanic by 2050. If you go to a museum, and don't see anyone who looks like you, from visitors to staff, and the boards are not reflecting the community, you may be less likely to come back, or even to go in the first place."

Marketing studies affirm the rather obvious fact that African Americans are more likely to attend events that are characterized as "Black themed" and events where Black people are well represented among performers. Studies of Latino attitudes toward museums show similar results. A report and survey by the Smithsonian American History Museum found second-generation Latinos surveyed had "very strong expectations that museums should include diverse staff, bilingual interpretation, Latino perspectives and some Latino themed content."

In Houston, our colleague, the late Peter Marzio of the Museum of Fine Arts (MFAH), started a Latin American department in response to the city's rapidly expanding Latino community. Peter also added several permanent Asian art galleries in response to Houston's growing and diverse Asian community. And he did not start these exhibitions and programs in some vacuum, but rather by engaging the local community and asking what they wanted. This has resulted in very strong local support, donations, and engagement. As an example, the Korean community donated over $2 million for a permanent art collection.

I turn now to the situation of those of us who are described in a Native American saying as holding up half of the sky—us women folk. Where do we stand in terms of women on museum staffs?

Among the museums in the Association of Art Museum Directors, women make up slightly less than 50 percent of the directors. However, of the 243 members of the Association of Art Museum Directors, there are only five African American women! It is also important to note that women lag behind men in directorships held at museums with budgets over $15 million. And women (primarily White women, given the paltry number of women of color) earn seventy-one cents to every dollar earned by male directors.

From the National Museum of Women in the Arts in Washington, DC, here are these facts:

- 51 percent of visual artists today are women.
- Over the past fifteen years, only 28 percent of museums' solo exhibitions spotlighted women (limited to eight selected museums).

- Only twenty-seven women are represented in the current edition of H. W. Janson's seminal textbook, *History of Art*, up from zero in the 1980s.
- Less than 3 percent of the artists in the modern section of the Metropolitan Museum of Art are women, but 83 percent of the nudes are women!

Calvert Investments discovered that companies whose commitment to diversity was viewed as "robust" were not only at a financial advantage but were also better positioned to generate long-term shareholder value. In addition, advocacy groups like Catalyst (a nonprofit organization that promotes inclusive workplaces for women) found that Fortune 500 companies with higher percentages of women board members significantly outperformed companies with fewer female members. And let us note that women have more philanthropic clout than ever before, consistently outgiving their male counterparts. Clearly, museums have something to gain by including more women on their staff, on their boards, and in their exhibitions.

The relationship between American museums and LGBTQ communities is similarly lopsided. Whatever the number of lesbian, gay, bisexual, and transgender individuals there are among museum professionals, such statistics are not available, American museums have paid grossly insufficient attention to artworks done by and about individuals of these communities.

The exhibition at the Smithsonian Portrait Gallery, *Hide/Seek: Difference and Desire in American Portraiture* (November 18, 2011–February 12, 2012), was the first mainstream museum exhibition to focus on themes of gender and sexuality in modern American portraiture. As you may recall, there was a major controversy around that exhibition when the Smithsonian removed a 1987 video about the suffering caused by AIDS. Many in the LGBTQ community—a community that had suffered disproportionately from the AIDS crisis—and some individuals from other communities felt this was an act of censorship. At the Smithsonian, conversations continue about what can be learned from that controversy, and how we can better steward the voices of marginalized populations when political blowback may be forthcoming.

We must also address the question of how inclusive our museums are in terms of exhibitions curated by and for differently abled people. Generally, museums do a fair job of adhering to legal requirements for accommodation, such as wheelchair ramps. And some museums are now creating ways that individuals who are visually impaired or blind can enjoy art works in museums. But fully including the disabled community means going beyond access to exhibits. We must ask ourselves to what extent our museums welcome disabled professional staff and artists, and the extent to which our museums accommodate and welcome people with invisible disabilities, like the neurodiversity of autism or dyslexia. Imagine the creativity we could ignite by commissioning a work of art for autistic children, a work that allowed for physical manipulation and soothing stimulation. Imagine the number of parents who would bring their children and become grateful patrons.

Finally, in terms of underrepresented groups, I pose this question: How are our museums doing in terms of igniting the interest of the folks that I respectfully, yet

playfully, call the young'uns? As you know, millennials are quite different from yes-
terday's museumgoers in how they see the world, how they engage with technology,
and how they pursue their interests. It is not being overly dramatic to say that unless
we make changes in our museums that will speak to the patterns and interests of
young people, when the middle-aged and older folks who are now our core visitors
go on off to glory, our museum galleries will be places in which there is a dwindling
number of visitors. We all know that our museums must become more technologi-
cally savvy if we are to court young adults whose electronic devices have become
extensions of their minds and bodies.

Not only is reaching out to the millennial generation important for cultivating
healthy visitorship, but it is critical for preparing the next generation of donors
and trustees. While the baby boomer generation has been the main source of charitable giving and philanthropic leadership for decades, the realities and habits of
the millennial generation are not the same as the current aging generation. From
a recent *TrendsWatch* report compiled by our American Alliance of Museums and
a recent *New York Times* article, "Wooing a New Generation of Museum Patrons,"
we learn this:

> While charitable giving in the United States has remained stable for the last 40 years,
> there is reason for concern. Boomers today control 70 percent of the nation's disposable
> income. Millennials don't yet have nearly as much cash on hand. And those who do are
> increasingly drawn to social, rather than artistic, causes.[1,2]

The fiscal reality of the millennial generation is not the same as the reality of
older generations. Tax laws are changing, and wealth is becoming increasingly concentrated, which will in turn affect the philanthropic habits and the focus on giving
of the younger generation. In addition, there may just be fewer wealthy patrons and
donors, making donor relations and cultivation a more critical and targeted effort.

Colleagues, when we pause to confront the need for far greater diversity in our
museums, in many ways, we are at the proverbial fork in the road. We must decide
if we will continue on our path so that our museums reflect the histories, cultures,
art, and science of only some of the many people who make up our nation and our
world, or if we will take the other path, which requires bravely cutting through old
habits and institutional resistance to inspire and create change.

If your museum is large or small, old or young, famous or not yet famous, the
need for seeking and sustaining diversity in your museums and in mine has never
been greater. If we are to be relevant in this ever-changing world, to stay artistically
and financially viable, all of our museums must boldly, indeed bodaciously, commit
to reenvisioning what takes place in our museums, to whom our museums belong,
and which colleagues have the privilege of telling important stories through the
power of science, history, culture, and art.

As members of AAM, you my colleagues are aware of efforts in this organization
to address issues of diversity in our museums. There are also programs initiated by
other museum organizations, like the Association of Art Museum Directors, and

by institutions like the Ford Foundation and the Andrew W. Mellon Foundation, to encourage far greater involvement of underrepresented groups in every facet of American museums.

In this city that was the birthplace of one of the greatest drum majors for justice in our nation's history, I ask us to commit to the task of bringing greater diversity to American museums and to the work that our museums do. And there is no time that is more appropriate for us to carry out this commitment than right now. So let us heed the counsel of Atlanta's son, Dr. Martin Luther King Jr., in terms of how we are to get this critical work done. He said, "If you can't fly, then run. If you can't run, then walk. If you can't walk, then crawl. But whatever you do, you have to keep moving forward."

If you are at all curious as to who in your organization is responsible for making our museums more representative of the diversity of our nation and our world, let me end by telling you a story that was a favorite of a great civil rights worker, Fannie Lou Hamer.

A group of boys decided to play hooky from school. To entertain themselves they decided to mess with a bird that one of the boys had caught. Soon, they were bored, so the ringleader said: "I know what we can do, we can find the old lady who lives up the road and ask her a question about this bird that she will never be able to answer. I will hold this bird behind my back and say, 'Old lady, old lady, this bird that I have behind my back, is it dead or is it alive?' If she says the bird is dead, I will release the bird so that it can fly away. But if she says that the bird is alive, I will crush it."

Convinced that the old lady would never be able to answer the question about the bird they gave each other high fives and fist bumps before starting out to find her. When they did, the ringleader called out: "Yo, old lady, you gonna answer my question?" The old lady with the warmth and gentleness that characterizes so many of our elders said, "My son, I will try."

Holding the bird behind his back, the ringleader said, "Old lady, this bird that I hold behind my back, is it dead or is it alive?"

The old lady, taking her own sweet time, simply replied: "It's in your hands!"

Sisters and brothers all, that is the answer: The responsibility for bringing far greater diversity into each and every one of our museums is in *your* hands, and in mine.

## NOTES

1. Philip M. Katz and Elizabeth E. Merritt, *TrendsWatch 2013: Back to the Future*, Center for the Future of Museums Project (Arlington, VA: American Alliance of Museums, 2013): 9, https://www.aam-us.org/wp-content/uploads/2018/04/trendswatch2013.pdf.

2. David Gelles, "Wooing a New Generation of Museum Patrons," *New York Times*, March 19, 2014, https://www.nytimes.com/2014/03/20/arts/artsspecial/wooing-a-new-generation -of-museum-patrons.html.

# 4

# Women's Locker Room Talk

## Gender and Leadership in Museums

*Kaywin Feldman*

*This essay was adapted from remarks delivered at the 2016 AAM Annual Meeting.*

I became a museum director at the age of twenty-eight. After I had been in the job for about three years, I interviewed for a slightly larger museum in Texas. During the meeting, the chair said to me, "You are far too young and far too female for a curator ever to report to you." And just to ensure that I remain mad about it, a few years ago I related the story to the then-director of this Texas museum, who was a strapping sixty-three-year-old former football player. Even though I had been the director of two larger art museums for the last twelve years when I spoke with him, he said, "Good advice, it is true."

I would like to address power, influence, and responsibility from a personal perspective. And I'm definitely going to play the woman card. I have encountered "far too young and far too female" for most of my twenty-two-year career as a museum director.

It is important to stress that I am grateful to the three museum boards in Fresno, Memphis, and Minneapolis that have hired me as their director. These boards bucked a trend in giving me a chance; I'm one of the lucky ones. I love my job and feel extremely fortunate to have had such a rewarding and stimulating career.

To get to where I am, I have done quite a bit of interviewing. I heard the exact same concern every time I was not hired—and even when I was hired: "we are worried that she doesn't have gravitas." I'd like to unpack gravitas for a moment. It was one of the key Roman virtues, along with *pietas, dignitas,* and *virtus* (which, incidentally, comes from *vir,* the Latin word for man). Gravitas signifies heft, seriousness, solemnity, and dignity. It is weighty and replete with importance. I have come to realize that it is also subconscious code for "male."

In fact, the dictionary gives the following two examples of "gravitas" in a sentence:

- A post for which he has the expertise and the gravitas
- A comic actress who lacks the gravitas for dramatic roles

Isn't that funny; the negative example of gravitas is female. The Urban Dictionary defines the word as "a part of the male anatomy," going on to say, for example, that the few female news anchors who are thought to possess gravitas are often assumed to be lesbians or described as shrill and therefore do not last long in their positions. Instead, American news anchorwomen are often offered "perky" as a substitute description.

Please understand that my problem isn't with the word "gravitas" itself, it is with the cowardly discrimination that hides behind the use of the word. It's this thinking:

Women don't have gravitas.
Leaders must have gravitas.
Women, therefore, can't be leaders.

The Minneapolis Institute of Art recently adopted a new brand, working with the design firm Pentagram. We had been in the lively and engaging process of fully defining and expressing our brand for the previous four years. Pentagram studied us and responded, "Your full name is too long. Luckily, your acronym is pronounceable. You're just saying your name wrong." Instead of being the MIA—Missing in Action or the Miami International Airport—they suggested we should be known as "Mia," which means "mine," "my own," or "beloved" in eight languages. Now that was compelling, but our team was concerned. At first no one articulated it, but the discomfort derived from Mia being a female name. Finally, one of our trustees voiced it: he didn't like Mia because "it is not strong. It's not classical or smart. It's just not serious." I pointed out that if our name spelled "SAM" or "TOM" he wouldn't have had the same reaction. What he was clearly saying, without realizing the gender implication, was that the name, a female name, didn't have gravitas.

In a *New York Times* article by Claire Cain Miller of March 18, 2016, Miller noted that when a profession that is largely male transitions to largely female, salaries decrease significantly, even after adjusting for education, experience, and geography. Overall, in fields where men are the majority, the median pay is 21 percent higher than in occupations with a majority of women. Miller proceeds to note that of the thirty highest-paying jobs, twenty-six are male-dominated. Of the thirty lowest-paying professions, twenty-three are female-dominated.

The implication of the studies cited in this article is that a job just can't be as serious, challenging, or sophisticated if it can be done by women, and therefore should receive lower compensation levels. After reading the article, I realized that this was one of the main reasons that many boards are reluctant to hire women directors. Deep down, male and female trustees fear that it would demean and debase their museum, and the profession, if a woman can do the job.

In the art museum field, about 45 percent of museum directors are female. That's great, and the number represents a dramatic increase in a relatively short period of time. But among the seventeen largest encyclopedic art museums, with budgets over $30 million, there are only two of us. A colleague noted that the Association of Art Museum Directors is replete with foreign accents, commenting that art museum boards are now importing men from abroad. This trend is particularly disturbing since in sheer numbers, women significantly dominate in the field of art history.

Boards do not explicitly decide that they want to hire a man; I truly believe that they approach searches with the best of intentions and are committed to diversity. But they think a director must exude silver-haired baritone aloof solemnity, and therefore they unwittingly rule out female applicants. This sort of underlying sexism is so much more insidious even than the trustee who once said directly to me that "things would go a lot better if you would do as you're told" (I was forty-three years old at the time).

Leadership qualities are equally found in women as in men, even if they look and sound a bit different. People debate whether men and women demonstrate different leadership qualities. I believe that often men and women do in fact have different approaches to leadership, although it is not an absolute, and often men demonstrate female qualities and vice versa. I am not advocating that any one style is the correct one, either. I feel strongly that we must acknowledge that there is often a difference and that a spectrum of effective leadership styles exists. The very best leaders are able to adapt and demonstrate leadership tools with agility, as the situation dictates.

A reason that women are perceived to lack gravitas is because they often demonstrate more of a human-centered leadership style. While they are not mutually exclusive, female leadership can appear more humanitarian, affectionate, helpful, warm, and sympathetic. Unfortunately, female human-centered leadership is often dismissed as simply "being nice," with all of the female identity baggage that this phrase entails. Being human-centered in one's leadership style, however, does not rule out also being decisive, strong, or holding others accountable.

The reason we perceive that women don't by nature demonstrate gravitas is because our society assumes that female human-centered leadership is at odds with male gravitas. The two styles imply this sort of duality:

| Gravitas | Human-Centered |
|---|---|
| Exclusive | Inclusive |
| Self-reliant | Solicitous |
| Independent | Generous |
| Polite | Gracious |
| Intelligent | Emotionally intelligent |
| Aloof | Congenial |
| Sophisticated | Enthusiastic |
| Powerful | Empowering others |

Psychologists who have studied the difference between male and female leadership styles have identified that men are agentic (assertive, competitive, and masterful) and women are communal (warm, compassionate, helpful, sympathetic, and collaborative). In a persuasive article by Alice Eagly and Linda Carli in the September 2007 edition of the *Harvard Business Review*, the authors pointed out that when surveyed, most people think the agentic form of leadership is the most successful, while most of us would rather work for a boss who is communal. Ultimately, however, it is the communal boss who is usually the most effective as a motivational leader who produces results. Furthermore, Eagly and Carli note that women leaders are often caught between a rock and hard place:

> As a result, women leaders find themselves in a double bind. If they are highly communal, they may be criticized for not being agentic enough. But if they are highly agentic, they may be criticized for lacking communion. Either way, they may leave the impression that they don't have "the right stuff" for powerful jobs.

The authors go on to note that men don't have the same "double bind." When assessing men who demonstrate behavior that is warm and friendly versus dominant and assertive, they are not penalized. Men, therefore, are seen positively regardless of their degree of warmth.

When I first started at Mia, we had a Nazi-era Holocaust claim that was eleven years old. It was a complicated case, and it had taken us a number of years to confirm that the painting on the museum's wall was indeed the one looted. After resolving that issue, museum leaders thought the heirs might have been compensated at some point because the picture had never disappeared from prominent public view. I came to the conclusion that we had never found proof of compensation, and that it was time to resolve the claim and return the picture to the heirs.

I felt miserable about the decision because our whole trustee committee was male, our lawyers were male, the curator was male, and my two predecessors who worked on the matter are male. The approach communicated to me was "we are going to win! We are going to fight this by not flinching." I too felt pressured to "fight it and win," as all of the men had been doing for eleven years. In returning the work, I was scared of the message—you hire a woman and what does she do in her first eight months but compromise? Where's the stamina?

I called an all-staff meeting so that I could personally tell the staff that we would be returning the painting, and I felt as though I had failed each one of them; after all, protecting the collection is the most basic job of a museum director. It was hard for me to stand before them and let them know I was giving up a painting. To my relief, the staff immediately joined together in a standing ovation, reassuring me that I had indeed done the right thing. The museum's trustees were also unanimously supportive. I resolved the issue with all of the seriousness, solemnity, and gravitas that are called for when righting the wrongs of a despicable Nazi-era crime.

Our society will not benefit from the leadership of female museum directors across all types of museums, of all sizes, until museum boards are more cognizant of their internal biases and tendency to dismiss female leadership styles. We all have the power, influence, and responsibility to recognize this bias when it is encountered so that our society's power structures cannot continue to hide behind implicit discrimination.

# Part 2

## DIVERSITY, EQUITY, ACCESSIBILITY, AND INCLUSION STRATEGIES

# 5

# Twin Threats

## How Ignorance and Instrumentality Create Inequality and Injustice

*Darren Walker*

Museums—and the work they illuminate—can have a transformative impact on a life. I grew up in Ames, a small town in Southeast Texas, where cultural institutions weren't exactly plentiful. But my grandmother, a domestic worker, would bring me art magazines and programs from the homes of the wealthy families for whom she worked. Page after page, hour after hour, I pored over those pages, and my mind visited worlds from which I otherwise would have been excluded. In many ways, because of these programs and pictures, my economic situation never limited my expectations for myself.

Later in life, as a young professional living and working in New York City, I was fortunate to explore and fall in love with many of the extraordinary museums. And now, as president of the Ford Foundation, my colleagues and I are staunch supporters of museums of every kind, whether they be the Smithsonian's National Museum of African American History and Culture, the Legacy Museum in Montgomery, Alabama, the Arab American Museum in Detroit, or the American Folk Art Museum in New York, among many others.

The Ford Foundation's long-standing support of museums is rooted in the belief that the arts inspire people of all ages to dream and imagine new possibilities—and if we truly want to address inequality, the kinds of experiences and opportunities that museums provide must be accessible to everyone.

Achieving this important objective requires all of us—funders, boards, and museum leadership alike—to overcome two major obstacles: the twin threats of ignorance and instrumentality.

## EXAMINING OUR OWN IGNORANCE

If you're reading this volume, you already are thinking about the value of diversity, equity, inclusion, and accessibility—and considering the many ways our museums and cultural institutions can address the issues in this field. That said, while it is easy to say we value equity and inclusion, even those of us with the best intentions can sometimes succumb to our own ignorance.

My Ford Foundation colleagues and I learned this the hard way. In June of 2015, we announced that the foundation would focus its work on addressing inequality in all its forms. After receiving hundreds of emails in response, I discovered we had failed to include a community that experiences untold inequality on a daily basis: the more than one billion people who live with some form of disability.

At the time, the Ford Foundation did not have a person with visible disabilities on our leadership team; we did not consider their specific needs when developing our strategy or provide those with physical disabilities with adequate access to our website, events, social media, or building. It's not something I had thought about before the issue was raised, and I was embarrassed that we had missed this. I took this feedback to heart, was grateful for their honesty, and began listening to leaders from across the disability movement about what Ford can do better—one of the first things we did was make sure our renovated building would be ADA accessible—and there's plenty of work still to do.

Disability is a perspective that must be considered in any conversation about diversity, equality, and accessibility, to be sure—but I also offer this story as a broader lesson for every kind of organization. One might believe that any institution—all our people, all our processes—would have checks and balances against individual biases. We might assume, as I did, that someone else will raise the issues that we individually overlook.

Unfortunately, no matter how good our intentions are, we all have biases, and we may unwittingly reinforce those biases in each other.

Without intentional work to get better, this dynamic between individual and institutional ignorance can replicate itself across an organization and affect what gets programmed and funded, who gets hired and asked to lead, even who feels welcome. That's why any organization composed of individuals must reflect on and meaningfully confront individual ignorance, privilege, bias, and the way gaps in our personal knowledge and experience can contribute to larger institutional disparities.

This is especially true for museums. As institutions that serve and inform the public, museums have a special obligation to be mindful about institutional ignorance—because it can have a direct impact on the perceptions and understanding of the people who traverse its halls and unintentionally perpetuate ignorance on a broader scale.

Each institution must be prepared to interrogate its own process and ask difficult questions—even when the answers might be uncomfortable or embarrassing: Who chooses what exhibits go on display? How do we think about accessibility? What viewpoints aren't being heard, or might get lost in a museum's bureaucracy? Who, if anyone, is in the position to challenge the ideas of this group? Who aren't we think-ing about, and how can we make sure their perspective is included?

One of my favorite things I've learned from the disability movement is the rallying cry, "Nothing about us without us." It's an incredibly profound mantra—especially for museums. Any space we hope to include a diverse range of people needs to be inviting, representative, and physically equipped to serve all those people equally. We cannot design an exhibit or display without considering who that work represents, whose story it tells, and how audiences might interact with it.

To make sure we do not succumb to institutional ignorance, we need to uplift diverse voices, acknowledge gaps in our own knowledge or experience, and be willing to listen, even when it is hard.

## EXPLAINING VALUE BEYOND INSTRUMENTALITY

Sometimes our institutions miss opportunities to be more inclusive and equal be-cause we are missing a perspective. Other times, our perspective might be missing the point. In addition to ignorance or implicit bias, one of the challenges that prevent institutions like museums from doing better on these issues is another pervasive problem that I call a mentality of instrumentality.

Too often, museums are evaluated based on their economic value, rather than their cultural value. A few years ago, I witnessed a stark example of this phenomenon. When Detroit's financial problems threatened both the city's retirees and the Detroit Institute of Arts (DIA), there were people pushing the museum to sell its collection.

Those who sought to sell off the museum's assets were not invested in the Detroit of 2020, of 2030, of 2050—let alone in the people who live there. They were not interested in the community that the museum served or making Detroit the kind of city where people would want to live. They ignored the relationship between the museum, the community, and the city's history, and instead saw the DIA as only a potential asset to be sold.

Fortunately, a group of foundations along with people from the city and state came together to save the DIA and Detroit. This extraordinary effort, and the in-credible sacrifice of many of the city's retirees, was a testament to a broader truth: museums have value for communities that cannot be expressed with a dollar value.

Economic arguments about museums and their value are not limited to extreme situations like the one in Detroit. They come up in nearly every conversation about the NEA or the NEH. What's more, this persistent market-thinking has determined and exacerbated many of the inequalities we currently see throughout the sector.

Take for example the issue of diversity on the boards of cultural institutions like museums. The statistics are startling. The 2017 Museum Board Leadership report by the American Alliance of Museums found that 5.2 percent of museum board members are African American, and only 3.4 are Hispanic or Latinx.[1] Of course, we know that this lack of diversity on museum boards reflects wealth inequality more broadly. Indeed, according to a 2016 report from the Institute for Policy Studies, "If average Black family wealth continues to grow at the same pace it has over the past three decades, it would take Black families 228 years to amass the same amount of wealth White families have today."[2]

It should not surprise us that having a wealthy board and having a diverse board might, at times, become competing priorities. For some institutions, the need for board members to be either massive donors or major fundraisers discourages the recruitment of people with diverse backgrounds and perspectives. It's yet another version of an argument I've often heard about museums themselves, that prioritizes capital over all other kinds of value.

While questions of capital might impact who sits on the board, they can also affect who is able to have a career in the field. It's no secret that employment opportunities—especially in leadership roles—are tied to experience. But for a long time, many formative experiences in the museum field were unpaid internships. When these entry-level jobs are unpaid, they become inaccessible to people from lower-income backgrounds and can perpetuate the disparities we see at every level.

Inclusion and access then are not limited to entrance to a museum, or even what kind of exhibits one chooses to feature; it must be considered on a holistic, structural, institutional level, from the interns to the board. If we are unwilling to invest in developing new talent or including new perspectives, we cannot be surprised when the people in leadership all look the same or enjoy the same privileges.

## DIVERSITY AS STRENGTH, DIVERSITY AS STRATEGY

When we succumb to our own ignorance, or prioritize capital over diversity, it's not just the wrong thing to do. It also weakens the organization. Institutions committed to diversity must be clear: diversity is not a sacrifice—it's a strength. Having more unique perspectives makes your organization more competent. It helps you see your organization more clearly and allows your institution to explore a broader range of possibility—in terms of being a more just organization, but also when it comes to new audiences or new artists, different areas of study, or different ways of coordinating a space. It's hard to conceptualize the extraordinary value of diversity until you have it—but in my experience, it cannot be overstated. And study after study confirms the power of diversity for organizations. But again, it's not enough to just value diversity—it also must be an explicit part of your strategy. And ironically, the less diverse your organization is, the more difficult that commitment can be.

Consider again the board of a museum. The board is tasked with shaping the strategic arc of the institution and ensuring it best serves the community. But if the board doesn't include anyone *from* that community, they'll miss out on critical, boots-on-the-ground experience that ought to inform the board's decisions. At the same time, if we want talented people from the communities we serve to help lead our museums, then we should invest in programs that will give them the experience they need to succeed in those roles.

For our part, at the Ford Foundation, we're not only supporting individual artists and museums, we're helping to build a pipeline of curators, critics, and museum professionals with perspectives and ideas that have been ignored or silenced throughout history. We're also working with museums and cultural institutions around the country that are committed to diversifying their own leadership and staff. Our hope is that talented leaders from more diverse backgrounds will help strengthen museums and ensure the future health and vibrancy of the arts in America.

Of course, improving diversity, inclusion, accessibility, and equity in museums is a journey. We hope that what we learn and discover can inspire other cultural institutions to evolve their practices. Together, we must be willing to openly discuss and dissect our ignorance and resist the temptations of instrumentality over inclusion.

## NOTES

1. BoardSource, *Museum Board Leadership 2017: A National Report* (Washington, DC: BoardSource, 2017), https://www.aam-us.org/wp-content/uploads/2018/01/eyizzp-download-the-report.pdf.

2. CFED and Institute for Policy Studies, *The Ever-Growing Gap: Without Change. African-American and Latino Families Won't Match White Wealth for Centuries* (Washington, DC: CFED and Institute for Policy Studies, 2016), https://www.ips-dc.org/wp-content/uploads/2016/08/The-Ever-Growing-Gap-CFED_IPS-Final-2.pdf.

# 6

# The Leadership Imperative

## Diversity, Equity, Accessibility, and Inclusion as Strategy

*Laura L. Lott*

The most important business strategy book every museum leader should read is the United States Census.

If you don't believe that your institution's strategy or business model needs to change, you will think differently after reading census and demographic reports and predictions. These data reveal that the country and its people are changing faster than most of us can comprehend.

An aging population of adults living longer, healthier lives; an influx of millennials or "digital natives" to the workforce and broader economy; a rapid trend toward majority-minority communities; a rise in interracial, interfaith, and same-gender households. We are living through a dizzying shift in who comprises the public that museums are meant to serve.

In many cases, museums of all types and sizes are not keeping pace with these rapid population changes. The nation's demographic shifts are not reflected in today's museums: who visits and supports museums, whose works and stories are told in museums, and who serves on museum boards and staffs. Slow to adjust their strategies and business models, some museum boards and other leaders are in complete denial about the changing world. Others understand and even welcome the changes, but feel helpless or don't know how to adjust with many other concurrent demands and ever-tightening budgets.

A few things are certain. In this changing world, museums' viability and financial sustainability depends largely on their ability to be relevant, magnetic, and inclusive.[1] Diversifying museums, in all aspects of their structures and programming, is both a moral imperative and a business necessity for survival, given museums' reliance on public funding and support in the face of changing constituencies. Thus, it is urgent that museum leaders—chief executives and board members—focus their attention on how to strategically and effectively bring diversity and inclusion into the culture of their museums.

# A HISTORY OF ELITISM

As any museum leader understands, the first step to making change is to understand the history of the challenges we face today. Like many other societal issues, insight and answers can be found in our history.

Some of the first museums in history date back to 500 B.C. in ancient Greece and Babylonia, when the wealthiest people of society collected and displayed artifacts from even further back in history. Fast-forward two thousand years, and it was still society's most wealthy who collected objects of all kinds and housed their encyclopedic collections in cabinets of curiosities.

In the more modern era, individuals and groups in Europe founded museum institutions to share their collections. These institutions were led by the affluent collectors themselves or people from their social networks. As a result, museum leaders comprised a community's most elite representatives with the knowledge, collections, and financial wealth needed to support a museum. Even the "public" museums were often accessible only to the middle and upper classes—and even then, people often had to apply in writing for admission to museums they wished to visit.

Museums today are still evolving from those private collections maintained by prominent, predominantly European-descendant individuals—to become more democratic, public institutions. The last several decades of museology has seen an encouraging paradigm shift in how museums approach their missions and values. There is a growing emphasis on education and accessibility, in all its forms. Progressive and successful leaders are moving beyond compliance related to the physical environment toward providing equitable access to everyone along the continuum of human ability and experience. There are concerted efforts to "decolonize" museums and to tell previously untold stories. Funding sources have broadened to include public support, funded by taxpayers and the general public. Today, museums are less "temples" for the elite and more education and community centers, anticipating and meeting community needs and striving for relevance to the broadest audience possible.

However, a 2,500-year history of elitism still haunts museums' practices, collections, funding models, and boardrooms. We still have a long way to go.

# OBLIGATION TO THE PUBLIC

Museums exist to make the world a better, more beautiful, more interesting and enlightened place. As storehouses of knowledge and protectors of history and culture, museums have long sought to house, preserve, and share important parts of our world—for current and future generations. Though they vary in their specific missions, collections, programs, and expertise, U.S.-based museums generally share a strong tradition and ongoing commitment of service to the public.

People revere museums. Not only does much of the public love visiting museums, research shows that the public trusts museums above most other sources of information. America's museums are considered the most trustworthy reliable source of information, rated higher than the news media, nonprofit researchers, the U.S. government, or even academic researchers.[2]

The results of a 2017 public opinion poll showed tremendous support for museums, including:[3]

- 97 percent of Americans believe that museums are educational assets for their communities.
- 89 percent believe that museums contribute important economic benefits to their community.
- 96 percent would approve of elected officials who took legislative action to support museums.
- 96 percent want federal funding for museums maintained or increased.

The data speaks for itself: whether urban or rural, conservative or liberal, or a museumgoer or not, Americans value the museums in their communities. The vast majority of Americans—many of whom rarely go to museums—want museums in their communities, want them to be successful, and support federal dollars spent on museums.

Why are these poll results noteworthy and meaningful?

Museums rely on this public support to survive. In addition to the history and tradition of museums, many of these institutions are built on legal requirements of service to the public. Governmental, quasi-governmental, and private nonprofit museums, which nowadays comprise the vast majority of museums in the United States, receive government and/or philanthropic funding contingent on their service to the public.

These critical sources of funding are often direct financial support in the form of grants or government budget allocations, as well as indirect support through tax exemption or government-funded and -subsidized land and buildings. None of these sources of public funding can be taken for granted.

Sadly, there are recent examples of museum budgets falling victim to financially struggling state and local governments. Whether the threat to sell the city-owned collections of the Detroit Institute of Arts, closing the Illinois State Museum for nine months as part of the state's budget battle, or eroding tax exemption through "payments in lieu of taxes" in the northeast United States, increasingly desperate government budgets are threatening public funding of museums.

Museums of all types should expect their service to the public to be scrutinized as these battles persist and intensify in the coming years. Some have even predicted that in the future there will be fewer organizations that will enjoy federal tax exemption. The entirety of the museum field must vigorously defend public funding for museums in all forms, in part by continually *proving* that museums are vital to the public good, inclusive of that public, and supported by the broadest public possible.

Museums that do not meet the demand to serve broader audiences will jeopardize their public financial support. This risk implores museum leaders to push for inclusivity as a matter of strategy and survival.

## FUTURE MUSEUM VISITORS AND FUNDERS

While the U.S. population is already one-third minority, heading toward majority non-white, today only 9 percent of the core visitors to museums are minorities and approximately 20 percent of museum employees are minorities.[4] This should be of great concern to museum leaders and board members for one simple reason: the group that has historically constituted the core audience for museums—non-Hispanic whites—will be a minority of the population. If museums do not successfully widen this core audience, the majority of the public will not be engaged with, and likely not supportive of, museums.

Varying rates of participation in museums by different racial and ethnic groups have been explored by researchers over decades with explanations ranging from fluctuating cultural traditions of museum-going and the influence of social networks to museum approaches that feel exclusionary and collections that overrepresent white, male, European-descendant artists, and their narratives.[5]

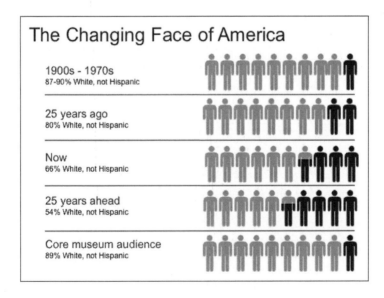

The Changing Face of America

1900s - 1970s
87-90% White, not Hispanic

25 years ago
80% White, not Hispanic

Now
66% White, not Hispanic

25 years ahead
54% White, not Hispanic

Core museum audience
89% White, not Hispanic

If museums want to be relevant to their communities, they must address these issues—and do so with deliberate, lasting, substantive change. One-off exhibitions or programs catered to more "diverse" audiences are not enough—and in fact tend to cause more damage to the institution's reputation as they are often inauthentic and short-sighted.

The shifting demographics of the United States are also disrupting philanthropic funding models of museums. Many museums tend to rely on a handful of wealthy donors, who often comprise their boards, friends groups, and advisory councils. In many museums, there is a quid-pro-quo that is unhealthy and unsustainable. In exchange for an often-prestigious leadership position in the community, such as a seat on the museum board, a trustee is expected to give large financial gifts. Museum leaders and trustees, under enormous pressure to raise more funding to endlessly grow their museums, argue they simply don't have the financial stability to diversify their boards and implement the cultural change that is required for diverse boards to be truly inclusive and successful. They too often equate diversifying the board with raising less money from board members. Above all, the argument goes, the museum needs funding—and inclusion can wait. This is not only a flawed governance model. It is a short-sighted strategy—and one where the end is in sight.

Economists are predicting an unprecedented transfer of wealth in the next few decades as baby boomers, the wealthiest generation in history, age and pass down a record-breaking $30 trillion to their heirs. Those set to inherit this wealth have different priorities and experiences, and they are likely to spend and give differently than previous generations, producing profound changes to the economy—and to the financial sustainability of museums.

Museums cannot take for granted that the next generation of wealth bearers will become museum members, serve on museum boards, or prioritize giving to museums in the same way as previous generations. Their loyalties and philanthropic priorities are being formed now. Are they actively engaged with your museum?

## DIVERSIFYING MUSEUM LEADERSHIP

As leadership teams recognize the necessity to adapt their organizations to the needs of our changing society, this includes examining who sits around the board-room table, which is often where critical decisions are made. Much has been written about the positive effects of boards with a diverse range of backgrounds, experiences, and perspectives represented across sectors. A nonprofit board is often expected to "represent" the organization's community to create accountability and form a link with the public. Diverse and inclusive leadership is better equipped to make policy and program decisions that authentically welcome more diverse staff, visitors, and partners.

And yet museum boards and leaders are often the least diverse aspects of museums. Within the past several years, there have been multiple surveys and studies within the field that reveal what many have feared about the perceived lack of diversity. The perception is a reality.

A 2017 cross-sector museum governance report showed 93 percent of both museum directors and board chairs identified as Caucasian. And 46 percent of museum boards surveyed were 100 percent white, containing no people of color.[6]

The picture of museum staff leadership, from directors and chief curators to heads of education and conservation, is not much better. In science centers and children's museums, 96.8 percent of CEOs identified as non-Hispanic white.[7] The Andrew W. Mellon Foundation's 2015 Art Museum Staff Demographic Survey showed 84 percent of staff leadership positions were held by non-Hispanic whites. Only 4 percent of these leaders identified as black, 3 percent as Hispanic white, and 3 percent "two or more races."[8]

The good news is that 77 percent of museum directors and 66 percent of board chairs surveyed believe diversity and inclusion are important to advancing their missions. They cite important reasons for prioritizing greater diversity and inclusion, including "enhancing the organization's standing with the general public," "understanding the museum's visitors," "developing creative solutions to new problems," and "understanding the changing environment from a broader perspective."[9] The same survey also showed that only 12 percent of museum directors indicated that they were satisfied with the racial and ethnic diversity of their boards.

The message from this report to the field was that museum leaders see diversity, or lack thereof, as a problem and something that needs to be fixed.

The bad news? Too few are prioritizing the necessary changes to produce different results. The data shows that fewer than one-third of museum leaders or boards have prioritized strategies to achieve a more diverse board or staff. Only 32 percent have evaluated and modified their recruitment efforts; 14 percent report that they have conducted diversity training; and only 10 percent indicate their boards have developed a plan of action to become more inclusive.

There is a real disconnect between perception and urgent action.

With so much at stake, why do museum leaders fail to consistently prioritize investments and actions in diversifying their staffs and boards, in ensuring inclusive and equitable treatment of staff, visitors, and other museum stakeholders? Why do they engage in the same hiring, governance, collections, and program strategies—but expect different results? Why is diversity and inclusion delegated to education or public engagement staff, where resources and authority for implementing substantive, lasting change is limited?

This work is hard and slow. Results are tenuous—requiring constant effort and reinforcement to endure. The issues are complex, and the battles are often exhausting. This is precisely why museum leaders must step up and prioritize the work. Furthermore, to truly face these herculean responsibilities, the American Alliance of Museums and its allies are obligated to help museums to broaden their leadership teams.

Understanding, planning for, and implementing fundamental changes in how museums engage and serve the changing public is vital for their relevance, sustainability, and viability. This must be at the heart of any museum's planning—and a top priority for its leadership.

## FIRST STEPS

So how does a board, with its director, get started?

First, make a commitment. Leadership must design a comprehensive diversity and inclusion policy. The American Alliance of Museums shares a comprehensive and continually evolving set of resources on its website to help, including template policies and plans for museums.

Then, as with any priority, museum leaders must work to understand the issues, reflect on their knowledge and blind spots, and identify resources to help. Unconscious bias training and basic cultural competence learning can be helpful.

Third, assess your museum's current situation. There are several strategic questions museum leaders must ask themselves to begin to understand the urgency of prioritizing diversity, equity, accessibility, and inclusion strategies, including:

- Is my museum inclusive of the broadest possible public? Do we reflect our community in all aspects of our structure and programming?
- Who comprises the board and staff of my museum? Whose voice is missing?
- Who are likely to be the future visitors, members, and funders of my museum?

With these first steps, museum leaders will identify some interventions with which they might need help—training on cultural change, model policies and procedures, and skilled facilitation of discussions with various museum stakeholders to open conversation.

Finally, museum leaders must hold themselves accountable, regularly measuring progress and ensuring long-term, substantive, and systemic change for our institutions and those we strive to serve—now and far into the future.

## NOTES

1. American Alliance of Museums, *Facing Change: Insights from the American Alliance of Museums' Diversity, Equity, Accessibility, and Inclusion Working Group* (Arlington, VA: American Alliance of Museums, 2018).

2. Reach Advisors, *Museums R+D Research Memo Number 1:8, Museums and Trust* (New York: Reach Advisors, 2015).

3. American Alliance of Museums and Wilkening Consulting, *Museums and Public Opinion 2017* (Arlington, VA: American Alliance of Museums, 2017).

4. Betty Farrell and Maria Medvedeva, *Demographic Transformation and the Future of Museums*, Center for the Future of Museums Project (Washington, DC: American Association of Museums, 2010).

5. James Chung, *Museums and Society 2034: Trends and Potential Futures*, Center for the Future of Museums Project (Washington, DC: American Association of Museums, 2008).

6. BoardSource, *Museum Board Leadership 2017: A National Report* (Washington, DC: BoardSource, 2017).

7. Association of Science-Technology Centers and Association of Children's Museums, *2016 Workforce Survey Report* (Washington, DC: Association of Science-Technology Centers, 2016).

8. Six percent identified as Asian, compared to 5 percent of the overall population.

9. BoardSource, *Museum Board*.

# 7

# History That Promotes Understanding in a Diverse Society

*Cinnamon Catlin-Legutko*

*This essay originally appeared in* The Future of History, *published by the Massachusetts Historical Society (2017).*

> In the past, Indians have had good reason to distrust and even to scorn the professional researcher. Too often have they misinterpreted the Indian history, misrepresented their way of life. It becomes necessary now to correct the record, to write the history as it should be written, to interpret correctly the aboriginal past.[1]
>
> —Rupert Costo, Cahuilla (1964)

For as long as I can remember, I've been in love with museums, all kinds of museums. I was a kid raised on public television, and on vacation our family traveled to museums and historic places. Each summer in Colorado we'd visit old mining towns and trace disappearing rail lines, imagining the past and wondering what life was like way back when. We would spend vacation time researching these towns in public libraries and archives, looking for photographs that showed them bustling with people. This was history that intrigued us, held our attention, and bound us together in family learning and adventure.

As I headed into my college years, I knew I wanted to work with precious collections, reveal the exciting stories that can be found in history, and inspire audiences to consider the human condition. As a museum leader, I've worked in a general history museum, a literary and Civil War historic site, and I am currently working in a Native history museum. My career was launched from an educational platform made up of training and study in cultural anthropology, archaeology, art history, and history.

I believe in museum spaces and their power to change lives, inspire movements, and challenge authority. And I have examples. The STEMinista Project at the

Michigan Science Center can inspire a girl to become a scientist and cure diseases of the future. The Lower East Side Tenement Museum can influence the national conversation around immigration through its dialogue-driven visitor experiences. A traveling exhibition called *Race: Are We So Different?* can change how museums and informal learning programs approach difficult conversations about race and society. This is a power that museums hold and can wield. However, I believe museum history and modern practice are terribly problematic for communities of color and, specific to my work and the examples presented below, harmful to Indigenous communities and their ancestors. Change is long overdue.

## MUSEUMS ARE COLONIZERS

> But one of the most important goals [of decolonizing museums], I believe, is to assist communities in their efforts to address the legacies of historical unresolved grief by speaking the hard truths of colonialism and thereby creating spaces for healing and understanding.[2]
>
> —Amy Lonetree (2012)

In the historic pattern of museum work, we find non-Indigenous people acquiring the belongings and the remains of people from other cultures. Museums are colonizing spaces. As Ho-Chunk scholar Amy Lonetree writes, "Museums can be very painful sites for Native peoples, as they are intimately tied to the colonization process."[3]

Historically, museums were built as temples of culture and art, reflecting images of Europe as the ideal. For many Euro-Americans, inclusion in a museum exhibition may instill pride and signify achievement. For colonized populations, it feels like being captured and isolated in a glass case or like being collected for display on a velvet-covered card. Natural history museums in particular used, and continue to use, classification systems to organize their contents: the "Hall of African Peoples," the "Hall of North American Indians" . . . you get the picture. Classifications may be convenient, but they lead to a troubling practice of "othering" by those who work in museums, people who are predominantly white, like me.

Let's unpack this term—colonization—for a minute. Colonization occurs when a population of invaders plants colonies in the homelands of other peoples. American colonialism is motivated by religious, political, and economic factors. People whose lands are colonized are in danger. The process leads to war, massacres, enslavement, and other atrocities. The real work of colonialism is the extraction of resources of colonized peoples. Cultures and human lives are always harmed and often destroyed during colonization. Always.

Right now, today, the United States remains in a colonial relationship with tribal communities. The invaders, the colonizers, are still here. This is a fact often overlooked by history practitioners and academics alike. As Susan Miller writes, "American historians have been loath to concede the point that the United States stands in a colonial relationship to the North American tribes whose homeland it claims." This is a key difference from Indigenous historians who have "no such aversion" to using "colonialism and colonization to explain relations between Indigenous peoples and nation-states."[4] To be clear, museums hold the spoils of colonialism: the artifacts and human remains of Native people.

The fields of history and anthropology have long crafted the narrative and the interpretation that describe Indigenous museum collections—fields dominated by Eurocentric, white voices and points of view. The history of museum representation of Native peoples begins with the development of anthropology as an academic field; modern representation stems from the late nineteenth and early twentieth centuries. Academics, especially anthropologists, earned accolades by systematically collecting American Indian material culture, that is, obtaining the authentic for museum collections.[5]

They were also removing the physical remains of Native people from execution burials, traditional burial grounds, and battlefields, and depositing the ancestors in museums. To this day U.S. collections hold the remains of an estimated half million Native American individuals, and European museums hold an equal number.[6] And while there is legislation in the United States to return the ancestors through the Native American Graves Protection and Repatriation Act, there is no such legislation (or the equivalent) requiring European repatriation.

So our perceptions of Native people and Indigenous cultures are shaped by the work of colonizers: people, like me, who are trained historians, anthropologists, and museums workers. What do the results look like in our memories and in our experiences today?

Whether as a young student or as an adult, we formulate a view of static, unchanging Indigenous cultures when we read the work of biased academic textbook writers and interact with museum exhibitions informed by the same biased voices. Certainly dioramas promote this view by depicting Indians as frozen in time and by displaying them in the same galleries as dinosaurs and other extinct animals.

Our memories may also recall Native objects defined and explained by Western scientific nomenclature and not by Indigenous categories of culture, worldview, and meaning. Exhibitions often remove the human story from the material culture on display by presenting artifacts as cold and lifeless when their meaning and purpose are intimately tied to human stories. Lastly, scholars and museum workers have homogenized Native communities into one pan-Indian group, disregarding the complexity and difference that well over five hundred Indigenous nations represent.[7]

These practices, which may have informed your memories, also dehumanize Native history and create colonizing museum spaces. In such places, emotional, spiritual, and physical harm is done when these colonized spaces and practices are not acknowledged and addressed. So it makes sense that many Native people would find American museums to be painful institutions.

## DECOLONIZING PRACTICE AT THE ABBE MUSEUM

Indigenous peoples have the right to practice and revitalize their cultural traditions and customs. This includes the right to maintain, protect and develop the past, present and future manifestations of their cultures, such as archaeological and historical sites, artefacts, designs, ceremonies, technologies and visual and performing arts and literature.[8]

—Article 11 of the United Nations Declaration
on the Rights of Indigenous Peoples (2007)

What is to be done? We need to decolonize museum spaces. Undoing the harm colonization has caused is the focus of our work at the Abbe Museum in Bar Harbor, Maine.

Founded in 1928, the museum's mission is to inspire new learning about the Wabanaki Nations with every visit. A historic confederacy of tribes, the Wabanaki are the Micmac, Maliseet, Abenaki, Passamaquoddy, and Penobscot. At the Abbe, their stories are shared through changing exhibitions, special events, teacher workshops, archaeology field schools, and craft workshops for children and adults. Native community members are actively engaged in all aspects of the museum, including policymaking as members of our board. The museum greets thirty thousand visitors each year with seven year-round staff members and about a dozen seasonal staff. In recent years, with broad community support, we have grown from a small trailside museum, privately operated within Acadia National Park, to include an exciting contemporary museum, opened in 2001 in the heart of downtown Bar Harbor.

Our organizational and strategic plans ask the overarching question, what can and should our museum do that is a service to Wabanaki people? Decolonization means, at a minimum, sharing governance structures and authority for the documentation and interpretation of Native culture. Borrowing again from Amy Lonetree, decolonizing practices at the Abbe are collaborative with tribal communities. This means that when an idea for a project or initiative is first conceived, we have a conversation with Native advisors and make sure it's a story or an activity that we have the right to share or pursue. We ask permission; we don't get halfway down the planning timeline and then check with Native advisors to learn how we're doing and if we're getting it right. And when ideas for an exhibit or program come to us from the tribal communities, we prioritize the ideas and work collaboratively to bring them to fruition. Native collaboration needs to occur at the beginning and be threaded throughout the life of the project.

A second characteristic of decolonizing museum practices is to privilege Native perspective and voice. The vast writings on the human experience are with little exception written by white academics and observers. When we begin to prioritize and privilege the writings and observations of Indigenous scholars and informants, the story broadens, expands, shifts, and introduces a clearer and nonoppressed perspective of Native history and culture. There is room to consider academic writing and research in this practice, but when there is conflict, both points of view may be presented, so long as the non-Indigenous research is not exposing sensitive information or causing harm to communities of people and their ancestors. And to this point, I have many Indigenous academic and advisor voices to credit: Amy Lonetree, Susan Miller, Taté Walker, Jamie Bissonette Lewey, Geo Neptune, Bonnie Newsom, and Darren Ranco. Their words shaped this article and influence my thinking on a regular basis.

Lastly, decolonizing museum practices include taking the full measure of history, which ensures truth-telling. Histories of Wabanaki people connect to today's challenges. Issues of water quality, hunting and fishing rights, and mascots are connected to the past and the present. When we present this full history we have a better opportunity to identify harmful statements and practices.

There are certainly museums across the United States and even around the globe that are incorporating decolonizing practices into their operations, but through our research we've found that their efforts are typically limited to exhibition development. We're concerned about exhibitions at the Abbe as well, but we're also looking at all of our operations—including governance structures, hiring practices, collections management, and educational programming—and creating decolonizing pathways. The Abbe Museum is committed to developing decolonizing museum practices that are informed by Wabanaki people and enforced by policies, managed by protocols, and overseen by inclusive governance structures. In addition, we will have other structures in place that will maintain the museum's commitment to decolonization regardless of the players involved—foremost among them the staff, trustees, and advisors.

## DEVELOPING THE SKILLS FOR DECOLONIZING WORK

> Dialogue . . . is a way of exploring the roots of the many crises that face humanity today. . . . In our modern culture men and women are able to interact with one another in many ways: they can sing, dance, or play together with little difficulty but their ability to talk together about subjects that matter deeply to them seems invariably to lead to dispute, division, and often to violence.[9]

—David Bohm, Donald Factor, and Peter Garett, *Dialogue: A Proposal* (1991)

Since 2013, the Abbe staff have been working closely with Sarah Pharaon from the International Coalition of Sites of Conscience (the Abbe is a member) to develop our skills in facilitated dialogue. We anticipated that our decolonizing commitment would require us to be able to have difficult conversations with each other, our board, and our museum audiences. In particular, our visitors would regularly throw us for a loop with questions such as "Are your Indians poor?" and "Can I touch an Indian?" While the visitors may not have intended to be hurtful when asking these questions, their impact is harmful for Native and non-Native staff members working the frontline audience interface. We wondered, how best could we transition questions such as these into new learning experiences that would broaden the visitors' understanding and minimize the potential for harm in the future?

We also observed that very often if a visitor was not alone, his or her companion would recognize that a question or action was rude or offensive or should be phrased differently, and would begin to mediate or correct the speaker. Dialogue was trying to happen on its own, and we were ill-prepared as a staff to engage.

Facilitated dialogue allows personal truths to come forward, be examined and valued, and be evaluated for harmful impact. The coalition describes the opportunity dialogue offers:

- "Dialogue gives equal value to the insights drawn from personal experience and the knowledge gained from intellectual study or external sources.
- Dialogue requires people to surface and examine the assumptions that inform their beliefs and actions. Dialogue invites a person to learn about him or herself while learning from others.
- The process of dialogue requires participants to establish, protect, and maintain a culture of mutual trust.
- The process of dialogue assumes that it is possible for two markedly different perspectives to coexist at the same time and therefore, rejects binary, either/or thinking."[10]

Fortunately for the staff, our board of trustees is committed to developing decolonizing practices and has evolved into a "learning board," hungry for readings and guest speakers to be part of our regular meetings.[11] The board could easily have been a limiting force as we dove into this training and its applications, but it was truly the opposite.

The team skill set is still a work in progress, affected by staff transitions and limited resources. We have piloted dialogue-based programs and are gradually embedding these skills into our work. Beginning in 2017, we will create and revise all educational programming to include dialogic elements, from opportunistic dialogues to intensive, guided dialogues. Facilitated dialogue places museumgoers at a shared table where they can see themselves as part of the story, either through personal connections or universal themes. This approach to relevance not only engenders support for history, anthropology, and museology; more importantly, it generates empathy in visitors when it connects the story to their worldview. When relevance is evident, oppressive and colonizing frameworks can be dissolved.

An intrinsic step in adopting facilitated dialogue in museum environments is to identify nonnegotiables. These specify what does not constitute acceptable conversation in your museum because it may be wholly untrue, even if it is commonly espoused by visitors, or because the topic is incredibly sensitive and harmful to some people and can act as a trigger. There is a wide host of reasons why selecting nonnegotiables is important for moving forward with difficult conversations. The coalition training also cautions that recognizing a nonnegotiable is to be done in a way that doesn't shut down dialogue—a delicate balance indeed and a process that was incredibly challenging for the Abbe staff. [12] Ultimately, we adopted three operational truths, or nonnegotiables:

- Dehumanizing thousands of generations of ancestors and Indigenous people is unacceptable and perpetuates intergenerational trauma.
- Colonization is an ongoing, harmful process.
- Wabanaki nations are sovereign nations. That sovereignty is inherent and cannot be taken or given away.

Once we put these words on a flipchart and confirmed that this is the truth of our work and that it is nonnegotiable, we all became surprisingly emotional. With these three truths in hand, we can navigate academia, practice, and visitor experiences while reducing harm to Indigenous people.

Of course, this isn't the only work we needed to do to be adept at decolonizing. At the same time as our study of facilitated dialogue, we submitted ourselves to racial bias training led by internationally known social justice activist Steve Wessler. Through his careful and experienced framework, we did self-work, looking at our biases and learning how to combat them and to interact in difficult situations when microaggressions, misrepresentations, stereotypes, and more are expressed in direct communication and overheard conversation in our museum space and personal life. Each year we offer this training to our seasonal staff as well as any new employees who have joined the professional staff.

Our training at the Abbe continues.[13] Most recently, trustee Jamie Bissonette Lewey, Abenaki, an accomplished healing and transformative justice facilitator and activist, led board and staff in a facilitated discussion she created on power sharing and museums. In two parts, the exercise first asked the question, "Where do museums have power in America?" The answers were wide-ranging and startling when viewed as a whole: museums have control of information and objects; they selectively disseminate information; they hold power over stories and interpretation; they determine what is and isn't "appropriate"; and they hold power over taste and aesthetics.

We followed this discussion by asking a second question, "What does power sharing look like?" The ideas we generated were motivational and achievable: a Native person would serve on all museum committees; Wabanaki cultural protocols are on par with museum best practices; academic and Native knowledge and scholarship are no longer adversarial; and our archaeology field school would be led by an Indigenous archaeologist. This discussion and others continue and are designed to reveal the work we have before us and to prioritize our next steps in service to Native people and their history, culture, and art.

When you choose to dive into decolonizing work, you must accept that you won't always get it right—there will be many missteps. Your personal need to espouse "correctness" isn't a good motivator, either. And in the scheme of museum operations, the decolonizing work won't appear as urgent as it needs to be. While the work will never be done, at the Abbe we've made the decision to no longer be complicit. We've made the decision to avoid creating harmful museum policies and practices. We've made the decision to commit to revising or reversing past practices that perpetuate harm. We've made the decision to change.

This article was adapted from a TEDxDirigo talk given on November 5, 2016, by the author (https://www.tedxdirigo.com/talks/we-must-decolonize-our-museums/).

## NOTES

1. Rupert Costo, "A Statement of Policy," *The Indian Historian* 1, no. 1 (1964): n.p.

2. Amy Lonetree, *Decolonizing Museums: Representing Native America in National and Tribal Museums* (Chapel Hill: University of North Carolina Press, 2012), 5.

3. Ibid., 1.

4. Susan Miller, "Native America Writes Back: The Origin of the Indigenous Paradigm in Historiography," *Wicazo Sa Review* 23, no. 2 (2008): 9–28.

5. Lonetree, *Decolonizing Museums*, 9–10.

6. Samuel J. Redman, *Bone Rooms* (Cambridge: Harvard University Press, 2016), 15.

7. Lonetree, *Decolonizing Museums*, 14.

8. General Assembly, *United Nations Declaration on the Rights of Indigenous People*, September 2007, 107th plenary meeting, http://www.un.org/esa/socdev/unpfii/documents/DRIPS_en.pdf.

9. David Bohm, Donald Factor, and Peter Garett, *Dialogue: A Proposal*, 1991, http://www.david-bohm.net/dialogue/dialogue_proposal.html.

10. International Coalition for the Sites of Conscience, *Facilitated Dialogue Training Materials*, 2013 and 2016.

11. How they became a learning board is a topic for another article. This was not an overnight transition and was not without serious bumps in the road.

12. International Coalition for the Sites of Conscience, 2013 and 2016.

13. The Abbe board and staff include regular Native representation and participation, but the percentage fluctuates from year to year. The board recently developed a protocol with the goal to reach Native/non-Native parity on the board by 2021.

# 8

## Pipeline Is a Verb

### Field Notes on the Spelman College Curatorial Studies Pilot Program

*Andrea Barnwell Brownlee*

In 2014, with support from the Mellon Foundation, Spelman College began piloting a Curatorial Studies Program. This project, a partnership between the Spelman College Museum of Fine Art and the Department of Art and Visual Culture, was created to introduce students in the Atlanta University Center (AUC) to curatorial practice as a specialized discipline of art history and, over time, help generate a pool of qualified African American museum professionals.[1,2] Students were eligible to apply if they were enrolled at AUC-affiliated institutions such as Spelman College, Morehouse College, and Clark Atlanta University. The launch of the Curatorial Studies Program solidified Spelman's commitment to addressing the persistent lack of diversity within museums.[3]

Museum staff and Department of Art and Visual Culture faculty were members of the Curatorial Studies Program Committee and they aided in establishing the short-term goals for the program as well as its measures for success. The initial committee consisted of myself along with Ayoka Chenzira, Ph.D., division chair for the arts; Makeba Dixon-Hill, curator of education; Arturo Lindsay, chair, Department of Art and Visual Culture (now retired); M. Akua McDaniel, Ph.D., associate professor of art history (now retired); Abayomi Ola, Ph.D., associate professor of art history; and Anne Collins Smith, curator of collections. Together through meetings, surveys, conversations with peers, and deliberations, we outlined three short-term goals for the program:

The first stipulation was to offer two courses during the 2015–2016 academic year. Mora Beauchamp-Byrd, Ph.D., a visiting assistant professor of art history, taught Introduction to Curatorial Studies, Mining the Museum, and seminars, which would serve as the foundation of the program.

Secondly, we aimed to match students with curators and other museum professionals who would give informed advice and help students make critical decisions about their academic and career pursuits.

And finally, the program was designed to direct students to paid internships in respected museums throughout the country for two consecutive summers. These opportunities would last for up to ten weeks and would allow students to work closely with curators on upcoming exhibitions and projects when class is not in session.

Ten students were selected to participate in the first installment of this two-year program. As the initial phase of the Curatorial Studies Program nears its conclusion, it is an ideal time to articulate the beliefs that informed our trajectory, so we must now evaluate the six strategies we employed and consider our options for the future.

Social media–driven movements such as #BlackLivesMatter and #MeToo, as well as countless documented examples of racially motivated injustices, underscore the critical need to address inequity and systematic oppression in society. The recent appointments of a white woman as the curator of African art at the Brooklyn Museum and a white man as the director the Metropolitan Museum of Art have provoked sharp criticism. Meanwhile, museums routinely cite an inability to identify, attract, select, and hire people of diverse backgrounds for leadership positions.

Within this context, the Spelman College Curatorial Studies Program committee is grounded in two core beliefs. Firstly, that the persistent challenge of diversifying museums and museum leadership relies on an interconnected network of solutions and demands a multitiered, results-driven approach. Not one institution or approach alone will work.[4] Secondly, we believe that most museum professionals want the field to be vastly more diverse than it is today. Our program, in part, relies on the idea that with inspired leadership, organizations will be able to take deliberate and perhaps unconventional steps that will yield significant change. Spelman is boldly and unapologetically pursuing this course with the expectation that in time many institutions will ultimately begin to take proactive steps and actively demonstrate that inclusion is as much of a priority as fundraising, board development, marketing, and other operating initiatives.

The often-proposed solution to the lack of diversity in museums is to create a pipeline. While directing the Spelman College Curatorial Studies Program, we began treating "pipeline" as a bold, deliberate, and overdue action, rather than a static underground vessel through which commodities and goods are moved and transported. The lessons learned that are offered here presuppose that identifying and hiring from a diverse pool of candidates demands that we reorder our way of thinking, remain focused on long-term investments, and develop clear strategies to guide, make room for, and welcome future generations of museum professionals. Our efforts are firmly rooted in the belief that we are creating viable pathways, which are productive strategies through which to advance the field.

## #1: PIPELINE WITH PURPOSE

Spelman is keenly aware that there is a great need to diversify every sector of the museum field. Specialized senior leadership positions that sorely lack in diversity include, but are not limited to, conservators, museum educators, registrars, development directors, finance officers, and human resource experts. However, rather than try to respond to these varied sectors, the committee's priority was to clearly define which specific challenge it could best address. Art history has been a sustained force in the Atlanta University Center since Hale Woodruff and Nancy Elizabeth Prophet established the Art Department in the 1940s. Spelman alumnae have succeeded in becoming arts leaders, art historians, and museum professionals. Spelman celebrates the growing impact of the Spelman College Museum of Fine Art and its mission to inspire both the Spelman community and the public through art by women of the African Diaspora.

To that end, the committee decided to maximize its strengths, focus on building upon its history, and create a program that will equip students with academic and preprofessional tools that will support their efforts to pursue graduate programs and curatorial careers.

## #2: PIPELINING RELIES ON PARTNERSHIPS

Feedback from student participants affirms that paid summer internships are among the most valuable components of the Curatorial Studies Program. Most participants in this program must earn income during the summer. Unpaid internships, which have historically served as barriers for many who are unable to take advantage of these basic entry points into the field, are simply not viable options for most of our students.[5] As such, we have called upon museum directors throughout the country and asked them to provide paid summer internships for at least one student in the program. Without fail, every director we asked took up the challenge—agreeing to pair a student with a supervising curator and ensuring that participants were fully engaged in substantial projects. Partnerships with institutions such as the following will continue to be the cornerstone of our program:

Samuel P. Harn Museum at the University of Florida (Gainesville)
Detroit Institute of Arts
Telfair Museums (Savannah, Georgia)
Crystal Bridges Museum of American Art (Bentonville, Arkansas)
Crocker Art Museum (Sacramento, California)
Smithsonian National Museum of African Art (Washington, DC)
Brooklyn Museum (New York)

These institutions along with the Whitney Museum of American Art, the Studio Museum in Harlem, and the Cleveland Museum of Art, which have long-standing, highly competitive summer programs where our students have been interns and fellows, have provided unparalleled opportunities, which Spelman College otherwise could not offer.

## #3: PIPELINE WITH PEERS

During the first year of the program, a student declared that she did not know she wanted to be a curator until she met one. That epiphany and the conversation that followed encouraged us to change our initial strategy in framing curatorial encounters. Rather than having the first in-depth introduction to the practice occur when students were paired with established curators, the program needed to facilitate worthwhile interactions that would allow students to spend quality time with curators and others in the field. We determined that in these early stages, students needed help to determine the scope of the curatorial profession, the demands of being a curator, as well as the field's expectations of those in such positions. To date, we have increased opportunities for students to have open conversations with leading art historians and curators in the field. Colleagues including Kirsten Pai Buick, Ph.D., associate professor of art history, University of New Mexico; Valerie Cassel Oliver, the Sydney and Frances Lewis Family Curator of Modern and Contemporary Art at the Virginia Museum of Fine Arts; Eddie Chambers, Ph.D., associate professor of art history at the University of Texas; Bridget R. Cooks, Ph.D., associate professor of art history and African American studies, and Desha Dauchan, lecturer of film and media studies at the University of California, Irvine; and Zoe Whitley, Ph.D., curator of international art at Tate Modern, have participated in a variety of forums including lectures, roundtable discussions, and informational interviews. This strategy has increased students' base knowledge of the profession, heightened their curiosity, and encouraged discoverability.

## #4: PIPELINE IN PRIVATE

Focusing on the matter at hand and working without the pressure of industry expectations and scrutiny of onlookers has proven to be a viable strategy for the program. While we have prescribed strategies for social media engagement—mainly as a vehicle to share highlights of the program's activities—our strategy has been to remain focused on the internal mechanisms of the program. And while many aspects of the program have gone well and as anticipated, we have identified some areas that require growth. For instance, we are still in the process of tweaking program activities and making critical hires so that the needs of the participants and long-term objectives can be met. The decision to be inward is, in many ways, counter to the current sociocultural environment that is focused on sound bites and instant gratification. However, this course of action supports our belief that some of the most notable examples of success do not make headlines. It also complements our impulse in this initial phase of the program to regularly evaluate the program and course-correct as needed.

## #5: PARENTS PLAY A KEY ROLE IN PIPELINING

The process of piloting this program has crystallized the fact that parents' perceptions about the arts and skepticism about professional mobility in the arts prevent many students from pursuing careers in the arts.[6] Misgivings about professional careers in the arts and questions such as "How will you ever make any money if you are an art major?" underscore the impact of parental persuasion. We have found that now more than ever we must double our efforts, provide a counternarrative, actively demonstrate that there are rewarding roles and careers within the field of art, and explore ways to make parents key allies in this endeavor.

## #6: PATHS BEYOND THE CLASSROOM

Another vital aspect of the program has been opportunities for participant travel. As travel is an expenditure that few students can afford, traveling with students has proven an essential benefit of the program. It has enabled us to emphasize that art should not be experienced passively. On one hand, students have access through their devices and are readily connected to endless resources. On the other hand, there is no substitute for experiencing art in person and meeting arts professionals face to face. Students have viewed several exhibitions and conducted studio visits in Atlanta as part of their courses. However, taking students to Washington, DC, to attend the James A. Porter Colloquium at Howard University; New Orleans to experience the biennial exhibition, Prospect 4; the opening symposium for *Soul of a Nation: Art in the Age of Black Power* at Crystal Bridges Museum of American Art in Bentonville, Arkansas; and an art intensive in New York has provided unique opportunities for the program to introduce students to curatorial practice in ways that cannot be simulated online or in a classroom. More importantly, such experiences have moved student participants beyond their comfort zones through personal encounters and engagements.

Facilitating conversations with collectors, artists, curators, professors, and art advisors including collector Darryl Atwell, M.D.; Valerie Cassel Oliver, the Sydney and Frances Lewis Family Curator of Modern and Contemporary Art at the Virginia Museum of Fine Arts; Rhea Combs, Ph.D., curator of film and photography at the National Museum of African American History and Culture (NMAAHC); Tuliza Fleming, Ph.D., curator, NMAAHC; Schwanda Rountree, art advisor; and artist Bill Gaskins have enlivened and informed our discussions. Planning for students to partake in special behind-the-scenes opportunities reinforces the reality that curatorial work requires a variety of skills.

## FROM PIPELINES TO PATHWAYS

The aforementioned strategies are logical, buoyed by clarity, and right-sized for this institution. By and large, the program has been met with great success and everyone who has invested in it is proud of its initial outcomes. Spelman anticipates building upon this foundational phase of the program as well as strengthening those areas we have identified for continued growth. The Mellon Foundation recently renewed its support for the Spelman College Curatorial Studies Program. Spelman was awarded a National Endowment for the Humanities Challenge Access Grant, which will enable the program to offer more student summer internships. As required, some of the resources from the NEH have been put into an endowment, which will support summer internships in perpetuity.

Mary Schmidt Campbell, Ph.D., the president of Spelman College, an art historian, former museum director, and cultural affairs commissioner of New York, has charged the college to reimagine what the arts at Spelman could ultimately become for the whole of its community and has enthusiastically championed the initiative. Dr. Ayoka Chenzira spearheaded the reconceptualization of the academic curriculum to best meet the needs of a twenty-first-century liberal arts institution. We are currently working closely with the Office of the President and Sharon Davies, the provost and vice president for academic affairs, to hire new faculty, expand the curriculum, and transform Curatorial Studies from a program to an academic minor.

Spelman College is in the process of solidifying our academic partnerships with Atlanta University Center institutions and working to create the Atlanta University Center Collaborative for the Study of Art History and Curatorial Studies. As a formal partnership between institutions within the consortium, it will offer much-needed academic opportunities for students attending Spelman, Clark Atlanta, and Morehouse. Most importantly, Spelman College is currently in conversation with potential funders and identifying others who will support our efforts to fortify our infrastructure.

Creating new pathways through the Curatorial Studies Program is an active, steady, and long process that will reap significant rewards. While not every student in the program will pursue graduate studies in art history or become a curator, we are confident that this program will develop individuals who will support art and art museums through a lifelong engagement with, membership to, and governance of such institutions. Likewise, we are certain that the program will introduce them to additional and related career paths within museums.

As we work to create avenues that welcome new voices and faces into the field, we are also declaring what inclusion looks like and considering what systems need to be in place to truly bring equity and diversity into the field. During this initial phase we have employed practical strategies, made significant strides, and reexamined preliminary findings. Our decisions have enabled us to remain nimble and incremental in our approach, yet demonstrably productive. It is noteworthy that attempts were made to diversify the field in the 1980s. While these efforts encouraged a few scholars and curators to enter the field and ultimately thrive, they were altogether temporary and did not greatly expand the field or increase access to it. Our current engagement affirms our commitment to building upon previous attempts, realizing tangible outcomes, and actively assessing and course correcting so that this program, in concert with other efforts, will have a transformative impact on the field for decades to come.

In this next phase of the Curatorial Studies Program, Spelman will redouble its efforts given the expanding framework both internally and externally. Internally, we remain focused on developing the Curatorial Studies Program to ensure that it is in full alignment with the college's strategic plan and its vision, which is to inspire teaching and learning in new and innovative ways. We are expanding our external partnerships, allowing for an expansion of resources and infrastructure from which to continuously build new opportunities for our students. Our commitment has never been more resolute. We have our sights firmly on shaping the museums of our future. The Curatorial Studies Program allows us the opportunity to be a catalyst and play a unique and integral role in the long-term and collective effort to make museums reflect the communities they serve.

## NOTES

1. In 2017, the Department in Art and Art History changed its name to the Department of Art and Visual Culture. This change signaled the college's emphasis on the expanding role of artists within historical and contemporary contexts. The department now also offers majors in documentary filmmaking and photography.

2. The Atlanta University Center, which also includes the Morehouse School of Medicine, is the largest association of historically Black colleges and universities.

3. Roger Schonfeld, Mariët Westermann, and Liam Sweeney, *The Andrew W. Mellon Foundation: Art Museum Demographic Survey* (New York: The Andrew W. Mellon Foundation, 2015). The often-cited report revealed that African Americans were less than 4 percent of museum leadership.

4. The Mellon Curatorial Fellowship and Summer Academy; the Diversifying Art Museum Leadership Initiative Curatorial Fellowship at the Pérez Art Museum Miami; the Winston and Carolyn Lowe Curatorial Fellow for Diversity in the Fine Arts at the Pennsylvania Academy of Fine Art; and the partnership between the Los Angeles County Museum of Art and the Herberger Institute for Design and the Arts at Arizona State University are noteworthy examples of programs that have been created to directly address this challenge.

5. Darren Walker, "Internships Are Not a Privilege," *New York Times*, July 5, 2016, https://www.nytimes.com/2016/07/05/opinion/breaking-a-cycle-that-allows-privilege-to-go-to-privileged.html.

6. Stephanie Storey, "To Succeed in Business, Major in Art History," *Huffington Post*, December 6, 2017, https://www.huffingtonpost.com/stephanie-storey/to-succeed-in-business-ma_b_10117802.html.

# 9

# Museums and ADA at 25

## Progress and Looking Ahead

*Beth Bienvenu*

*This essay was originally published in the September/October 2015 issue of* Museum, *published by the American Alliance of Museums.*

Our country celebrated the twenty-fifth anniversary of the passage of the Americans with Disabilities Act (ADA) in 2005 with commemorations, concerts, festivals, parades, social media conversations, and gala events. People took time to reflect on how far our country has come in ensuring full inclusion for people with disabilities. In the past quarter of a century, there has been an increase in opportunities for employment, education, transportation, healthcare, and participation in public life, as well as significant progress in terms of acceptance, attitudes, and perceptions about disability.

Within the cultural sector specifically, there has been progress for inclusion of people with disabilities. Museums have been steadily incorporating accommodations and programs that ensure inclusion for all visitors and participants. For people with vision disabilities, museums are using audio guides, large-print labels and materials, and content in braille, as well as tactile tours, models, and maps. For people who are deaf or hard of hearing, institutions offer captioned video, sign-language interpreted tours, assistive listening devices, real-time captioning, and sign-language interpretation. Museums are also paying more attention to physical access by ensuring wheelchair access to all physical spaces and installing exhibits and displays at heights that accommodate people in wheelchairs or those of short stature. Additionally, museums are more apt to offer seating options throughout galleries and have increased accessible seating in auditoriums.

Museums have also responded to particular conditions and circumstances as evidenced in new partnerships with the autism and Alzheimer's communities. Specifically, many museums offer visiting times for families with members on the autism spectrum when galleries are less crowded, special materials to help orient new audiences, and educational programs for people with dementia and their caregivers.

Many of these innovations in accessibility are due to the passage of the ADA in 1990, but the advocacy work began much earlier. When the Rehabilitation Act was passed in 1973, federal agencies were required to make their activities, and those that they fund, accessible to individuals that receive their benefits. This meant that museums receiving funds from federal agencies such as the National Endowment for the Arts (NEA), the National Endowment for the Humanities (NEH), the Institute of Museum and Library Services (IMLS), and the National Aeronautics and Space Administration (NASA) had to begin looking at how they welcomed visitors with disabilities.

Since the 1970s, the NEA has educated its grantees about these requirements, while also working with its network of state arts agencies to help them interpret how best to assist cultural organizations with the accessibility requirements. The NEA published a handbook called *Design for Accessibility: A Cultural Administrator's Handbook*, which provided easy-to-use information and resources on making programs and facilities accessible. The most recent version, published in 2003, is still used as a reference guide in museums across the country.

The NEA also partnered with the Smithsonian Institution and other museums to educate the museum field and provide resources for museum and exhibit accessibility. The Smithsonian took a leadership role in not only ensuring accessibility in its own programs and exhibits but by guiding science, art, culture, and history museums across the country through its various publications and resources, including the Smithsonian's *Guide to Accessible Exhibit Design*. The NEA worked with early champions of museum accessibility, including the Metropolitan Museum of Art, Boston's Museum of Science, and the Museum of Modern Art, to incorporate access and inclusion programs. Additionally, the NEA worked with the Graphic Artists Guild to develop a set of accessibility symbols, used in museums across the country; helped build the field of universal design; and was the first to work with museums to provide audio description of art for visitors with vision disabilities.

Despite such efforts, people with disabilities are still underrepresented in museum visitorship. A recent *Survey of Public Participation in the Arts* conducted by the NEA finds that adults with disabilities comprise less than 7 percent of all adults attending performing arts events or visiting art museums or galleries, as surveyed in 2012. The data also reveal that 21 percent of all adults visited an art museum or gallery, but only 11 percent of adults with disabilities made such a visit.

According to the Census Bureau, the baby boom population is turning sixty-five at a rate of ten thousand per day, and by 2030, 20 percent of the U.S. population will be over sixty-five, which will potentially increase the number of people with diminished eyesight, hearing, mobility, and cognition. In addition, according to the 2013 American Community Survey, there are 3.6 million veterans with service-related disabilities, and more people with disabilities are living independently in communities, increasing the potential audience of museum visitors.

Museums can benefit from attracting and retaining this valuable pool of visitors. Although museums have worked to increase their audiences of people with disabilities, there is still much to be done to involve those with disabilities in the curatorial, content, and decision-making activities of museums. Such a gap is noted by performer and activist Mat Fraser in his exhibit and performance piece, *Cabinet of Curiosities: How Disability Was Kept in a Box*. Fraser addresses this issue by challenging museums to question their view of people with disabilities as objects of exhibit and display, and to include their voices and experience in the work of the museum. As evidenced by the disability rights movement's slogans, "nothing about us without us" and "nothing without us," people with disabilities should be included as curators, exhibit designers, artists, historians, scientists, administrative staff, Web and application developers, and volunteers. They need to be a part of the conversation and the work of museums.

Leading the way in this regard is the DisArt Festival, launched in Grand Rapids, Michigan, this past spring. The festival's goals are to change perceptions and ignite conversations about disability and how it informs artistic practice. The festival and its follow-up activities have drawn more than twenty thousand visitors, featuring hundreds of artists and community members with disabilities. The festival's success was due in part to its many community partners, including the Urban Institute for Contemporary Arts and the Grand Rapids Art Museum. The festival's centerpiece was an exhibit curated by Amanda Cachia and funded by the NEA, called *The Art of the Lived Experiment*. The exhibition, initially presented at DaDa Fest in Liverpool, England, featured more than nineteen U.S. and international artists whose sculpture, video, painting, drawing, photography, ceramics, and performance creatively examined disability from an experimental point of view and addressed the uncertainty and change in both art and life. Through this exhibit and numerous additional exhibits, films, and community events, the DisArt festival succeeded in its mission to change perceptions of disability, effectively involving those with disabilities in all facets of the event.

What else can museums do to ensure full inclusion? The options are unlimited, but to name just a few:

- Consider the legal requirements and design standards set by the ADA as merely the *minimum* standard and expand efforts to ensure full access and inclusion for everyone.
- Incorporate universal design principles throughout the museum, ensuring that exhibits and facilities are designed to be accessed by all people, to the greatest extent possible, without the need for adaptation or specialized design.
- Consider accessibility from the start when developing and designing exhibits and programs, not as an afterthought.
- Incorporate the best practices listed at the beginning of this article throughout the museum experience.
- Work with curators and exhibit designers to design exhibits that are accessible to not only those with physical disabilities, but also those with sensory or brain-based disabilities.

- Pay attention to exhibit and display heights and font sizes to enable viewing and engagement for people of all abilities.
- Establish an advisory board of people with disabilities to advise on access and inclusion.
- Partner with local disability organizations to help inform your museum's work and develop new audiences.
- Train all staff to be fully aware of accessibility requirements and how to provide accommodations, rather than relying on one person or department.
- Take affirmative steps to recruit staff and volunteers with disabilities.
- Work with local college and university disability offices to recruit interns and graduates with disabilities.

The future offers many opportunities to expand access through technologies such as 3D printing, mobile applications, and new adaptive devices, as well as partnerships with the disability community and design with disability in mind from the start. Disability is a natural part of human life and offers a broad window into the human experience, from the perspective of the arts, culture, science, technology, and history. It is a perspective that museums should embrace.

# 10

# Catalyzing Inclusion

## Steps toward Sustainability in Museums

*Natanya Khashan*

Museums are not living up to their social responsibility; when asked to justify themselves and their roles in communities, many museums struggle to make a sound. This inability to demonstrate their relevance to their communities diminishes perceived value and increases turbulence. The twenty-first century has brought unforeseen challenges to the traditional museum model. We are in a time of rapidly shifting demographics, uncertain funding, an increased demand in attention to the needs of consumers, and a growing experience economy (whereby there is an increase in purchase of experiences over goods).

## UNCERTAIN FUNDING AND THE EXPERIENCE ECONOMY

Government funding for museums has not kept pace with inflation, requiring museums to rely more heavily on earned income.[1] This presents a Catch-22, as to rely on earned income, museums will have to expand their current audience base and reach out to a wider population than they have in the past. The explosion of the Internet and social media has increased consumer demand to pay for experiences, particularly in their local communities. The experience economy has prevailed in the United States; within this framework, the dominant offering is an experience that is memorable, participatory, and helps individuals connect to others. Businesses capable of fulfilling this need have a strong advantage in our modern marketplace, and museums are not exempt. In fact, the market demands that museums foster personal, meaningful connections with individuals and communities. To make those connections, museums must become inclusive, open spaces that are welcoming to their neighbors. Museums are so trusted by the public that they often serve as institutions that can function as a community's safe space, making museums the opportune place to learn, be entertained, experience new things, and socialize. Museums can utilize their collections to build meaningful experiences for visitors, their educational programming to make connections for individuals, and their resources to promote social inclusion and openness in their communities.

## SHIFTING DEMOGRAPHICS

Rapidly shifting demographics have threatened museum relevancy in profound ways because as the demographics of the United States continue to change, the traditional visitor profile remains the same: non-Hispanic whites with high levels of education and income.[2] With the continued growth of minority groups in the United States and of minority-majority cities, the museum visitor profile must similarly evolve to reflect current demographics. To do so, museums must begin to pay more attention to the audiences not coming in through their doors.

The challenges facing museums as they strive to achieve greater social inclusion are both rooted in their histories and a result of pervasive attitudes that museums primarily serve the well-educated, wealthy, and white. The assumption that excellence is antithetical to community engagement echoes the Eurocentricity museums need to fight if they are to retain their relevancy. It is dangerous to equate non-European work with work of a lesser quality. If a museum expects a population to engage with their institution, it must represent that group's cultural expression and point of view.

## THE NEEDS OF CONSUMERS

Facing the obstacle of retaining relevancy, museums must adapt to the demand of creating closer ties to their communities and serving the needs of their neighbors rather than the needs of their bureaucracy. Museums risk perpetuating social exclusion and exacerbating social disadvantage and injustice if they continue to operate with the same framework they have been built upon.[3] This lack of social equity manifests in the museum through lack of representation of minority groups in staffing, exhibitions, and programming.

Museums need to become community citizens: entities beyond their stature as buildings and collections. To rightfully claim their programming as sustainable for the foreseeable future, they must focus on community involvement and provide active resources for all, not a chosen few. Building consensus around community citizenry across board and staff members is required for sustainability and relevancy. Through commitment to looking outward and facilitating open dialogues with community members, every museum's value can become intangible.

The variety of public uses for the museum should be celebrated and can be essential to the field. Social inclusion practices in museums can promote tolerance and new perspectives via representation of different cultures through the display of objects and other media, thereby forming a bridge in our fractured and divided society. Visitors can bring and utilize their personal histories and associations to the museum, creating new meanings on those objects, and leave with a unique, new experience. Museums can reinforce connections within communities by providing a space to meet and facilitate conversation with others, thereby decreasing social isolation.[4]

## WHAT MUSEUMS CAN LEARN FROM THE COMPETITION

When it comes to tapping into the experience economy and maintaining relevance among shifting demographics, museums face intense competition with concerts, festivals, sporting events, the performing arts, amusement parks, and many more regularly held events that are experiential whether by nature or by design. But the example set by libraries, which are situated in a similar position to museums in their position as a city landmark, their open spaces, and educational missions, but who enjoy higher and more diverse attendance than museums, can help elucidate for museums how to leverage experiences that resonate with communities. According to the 2012 Pew Research Center Study, "How Americans Value Public Libraries in Their Communities," 54 percent of Americans over the age of sixteen had visited a library in the past year. The percentage was nearly equal (within one to two percentage points) between non-Hispanic whites, blacks, Hispanics, and Asian Americans. The National Endowment for the Arts' 2012 Survey of Public Participation in the Arts found that only 21 percent of Americans had attended an art museum or gallery in the past year. Of this 21 percent, 24.1 percent identified as white, 11.9 percent as African American, 14.3 percent as Hispanic, and 21.2 percent as others.[5] If libraries and museums are both situated in similar positions to the American public, why are these demographics drastically different?

According to the American Library Association, libraries are continuously adapting to meet the needs of their communities by creating maker spaces, providing workshops relevant to those in their community, and serving as small business centers.[6] The difference between museums and libraries across the United States is in the willingness to act with timeliness to the changes and needs of their communities. They actively seek out opportunities to promote educational attainment and social inclusion. As a result, they have experienced consistency in their attendance numbers and demographics and are representative of the United States rather than a specific subset of the population.

Museums' failure to be community anchors and tap into the experience economy is disheartening as they actually have a number of advantages over their competitors in the marketplace, namely:

1. Museums often serve as landmarks in cities, making the act of visiting a museum an experience within itself.

2. Unlike for-profit corporations, museums build trust with those in the community as mission-driven, nonprofit organizations. This trust leads to social capital, which then solidifies the museum as a community mainstay.
3. Museums are uniquely positioned between the academic world and the public, allowing them to create unique programs that enrich community conversations and situate them in a larger context. They can serve as the bridge between academic thought and public discourse in a way few other institutions can.
4. Museums have an inherent value and significance. People generally believe that museums are valuable, although many have not felt the value personally.
5. As nonprofit institutions, museums have volunteers, which is advantageous beyond the financial implications. Volunteers, when well-treated, trained, and recognized, can serve as community ambassadors for the museum.
6. Museums are holders of unique objects that describe the past, the present, and in many cases, the future. These objects are capable of sparking conversations among strangers, connecting people to one another, and creating memorable experiences.

## RECOMMENDATIONS

Given the above advantages, museums can strategically harness their strengths to become community anchors that foster social inclusion while generating enough earned income to become sustainable and maintain relevancy. The recommendations below will help museums foster diversity, inclusion, and equity at multiple levels of their operations.

To fully capitalize upon these advantages, museums must reframe their relationship with their visitors and communities. No longer stagnant recipients of museums' choices, patrons today expect their visits to be dynamic, engaging, and shaped with consideration of what is important to them. Content therefore becomes irrelevant if based on assumptions about, rather than the knowledge of, a community's needs.

To harness that knowledge, museums need to extend beyond traditional forms of research beginning with the identification of internal or external factors that unite a group of people within the community. Examples include where people live, work, play, or worship as well as hobbies, interests, values, gender and sexual orientation, race, ethnicity, disabilities, and age. Who within the museum—whether staff members, board members, donors, or partner institutions—can offer further insight into these community characteristics? And can the museum use exploratory methods such as forming advisory committees and focus groups, conducting one-on-one interviews, attending community events, and engaging community leaders to further enrich that understanding? This knowledge should then be used to inform not only exhibitions and experiences, but also operational decisions like staffing, board membership, and other functions. Only through concerted efforts to ensure that members of the community are represented at all levels of museum operations—from the museum board to volunteer staff—can a museum fully solidify its institutional value in a rapidly changing landscape.

The importance of board diversity cannot be understated for museums. It remains one of the most progressive and effective ways to institutionally ensure social inclusion has a role in a museum. Museum boards are typically homogeneous, self-selected for their fundraising acumen, corporate ties, or business experience. While these qualities are important, it is equally important to ensure a diversity of attributes including gender, race, disabilities, generational cohorts, background, geographic location, and community reach. Boardrooms must reflect the diversity of culture, thinking, and perspectives—not tokenism—required to challenge routine while monitoring risks. Consistent gap analyses can provide insight into characteristics that are lacking for future board recruitment and a diversity policy that addresses the need for wide-ranging perspectives in board membership.

However, diversity without inclusionary practices can leave a board feeling fractured and dampen its leadership. For a diverse board to be an effective mechanism of change in museum practices, board members will be challenged to move outside their comfort zone and examine their own biases. This is a slow process if it is to be done right, but the time it takes to do so will allow the board to act in a collaborative and cohesive manner. The result will be consistent messaging from the director and board level about the importance of social inclusion, which is critical for adoption at all levels of the museum.

Following board representation, museums must also proactively hire people who reflect the diversity of their communities. If staff members are not diverse, museums risk stereotyping or tokenism when presenting different cultures, values, and interests to the public. A hiring process centered on fostering diversity boosts the museum's credibility and influence, empowering staff members to make the museum relevant to their communities.[7]

Growing the candidate pool can result from cultivating external relationships with community partners and educational institutions, hiring outside of the museums field, and broadening the skill sets specific roles require to diversify the perspectives and insights of a staff. And building a diverse pipeline of candidates starts with paid internships to ensure that no doors are closed on those who can't afford to work unpaid.

This pipeline is equally important to entry-level museum roles such as that of docents, security, and other front-line staff. People who serve in these roles are the face of the museum for visitors. As the only personal contact visitors have during their time at a museum, on-the-floor employees represent the museum to those visitors. A community member should not visit a museum to find that no one serving on the staff of the museum looks like or can relate to them, or alternatively that only janitorial and security staff look like them. Having a more diverse staff on the floor of the museum allows people of diverse backgrounds to feel that the museum has their interests at heart and employs people like them.

Yet it is not enough for a museum to merely employ diverse floor staff; it must ensure that these personnel feel invested in the museum's mission through inclusion in staff meetings, leadership trainings, and other advancement opportunities. If all employees do not feel as though they are part of the museum's culture, not only do museums lose out on vital sources of innovation and new ideas, the employees' unhappiness will translate to visitors of the museum and can lead to poor customer service for visitors, ruining their experience and lessening the chance that they will return. Alternatively, if museums provide high-level training to docents, security guards, and other floor personnel that focuses on good storytelling, visitor interaction, and inviting questions, visitors will walk away with a positive intellectual and emotional impression of the museum. And museums will likely find themselves increasing their relevancy with small suggestions from these staff members, who have in-depth knowledge of their communities.

In addition to more diverse boards and personnel, advisory committees can be formed with participants who work for social service organizations, churches, city councils, public libraries, or local businesses, as well as community historians, journalists, or government-community liaisons. In recent years, the Bronx Museum has employed advisory councils to great effect. On their selection process, Lauren Click, director of community and public programs from 2010 to 2017, says, "We look for people that are very thoughtful, plugged in, and interested in their community." Many of the museum's programs informed by this deliberately selected Community Advisory Council (CAC) go on to attract unprecedentedly large attendance. Click goes on to describe the broader impact of the CAC on the Bronx Museum: "Our attendance has almost quadrupled in the past five years from about 30,000 to now over 100,000 people per year and a large part of that is due to the CAC."[8] Museums can assess the success of their advisory committees by considering members' active participation and attendance to meetings and programs, involvement in the recruitment of new members, and lasting engagement with the museum after the conclusion of their tenure.

In terms of innovation and relevancy, museums will be hard pressed to find a more honest source of information than teenagers. Teenagers can bring a new perspective into the museum, and their participation is crucial to sustaining the attendance of younger audiences as they move into adulthood. Teen councils involving students between the ages of thirteen and seventeen can have tremendous success when executed well.

There are several recommendations museums should consider when structuring teen councils. Groups must be small enough so all participants know each other's names and rely on each other. The group's diversity is an important consideration with characteristics including demographics, school affiliations, interests, career aspirations, and personality traits. Weekly meetings should be held on the same day and time to maintain consistent attendance. Additionally, as many students are expected to work to assist in providing income for their families, museums should consider financial incentives for teens. If the museum has a large community of immigrant students whose legal status needs to be considered, financial incentives may not be the best choice. In these circumstances, or if the museum is incapable of paying their students for their participation, providing food and supporting transportation costs is recommended.[9]

In short, the crucial service committees should serve is to open the museum to a wider audience. It is also important that if the museum is receiving this specialized insight from committee members, those members feel their input is respected, acted on, and they feel their commitment is valuable to them and the museum.

## EVALUATION OF SOCIAL INCLUSION PRACTICES

Though evaluation of social inclusion efforts is nuanced, and benchmarks are idiosyncratic, it is not impossible to do and do well. Options include evaluating the number of partners the museum works with over time, how much resistance there may be for a museum to become more actively involved outside of its walls inside its community, if museum staff members are implementing new learnings, and if the museum is noticing support from local agencies. Common quantitative evaluation methods such as attendance tracking should be balanced with dynamic qualitative methods such as feedback from focus groups, interviews, and surveys or behavior goals to assess the level and depth of participation in a program. For example, attendance numbers can be recorded for quantitative data while the level and depth of participation can be documented for qualitative data. Each program will require a different set of questions that need to be asked and museum staff will likely need to develop a unique methodology to discover indicators, patterns, or answers. To ensure that this process does not become onerous, evaluation methods can be iterative, each built upon the last.

To determine if specific programs or the museum is accomplishing engagement with the community, a museum should consider tracking through behavioral observation such as which activities people participate in, how long they stay in the museum, and through visitor surveys.[10] A long-term tracking method option includes measuring how many people in the targeted community become members, volunteers, and donors, who is attending public meetings, and who is providing feedback when asked.[11] These methods of evaluating the effectiveness of a museum's engagement with a new community can provide valuable insight, informing the museum on its successes and where it can improve.

In summary, museums must take a proactive approach to their role within a changing landscape, understanding they are dynamic organizations rather than static institutions, to continue to thrive now and into the future. Honest assessments, deliberate decision-making, and realistic goal-setting will enable museums to make authentic progress toward increased social inclusion. Through such heightened self-reflection and proactive efforts, museums can ensure that they remain invaluable assets to their communities.

68 Natanya Khashan

# NOTES

1. Stephen E. Weil, *Making Museums Matter* (Washington, DC: Smithsonian Institution, 2002).

2. Betty Farrell and Maria Medvedeva, *Demographic Transformation and the Future of Museums*, Center for the Future of Museums Project (Washington, DC: American Association of Museums, 2010), 1–41.

3. Richard Sandell, "Museums as Agents of Social Inclusion," *Museum Management and Curatorship* 17, no. 4 (1998): 401–18.

4. Lois H. Silverman, *The Social Work of Museums* (London: Routledge, 2010).

5. National Endowment for the Arts, *NEA Research Report #57 September 2013*, "How a Nation Engages with Art: Highlights from the 2012 Survey of Public Participation in the Arts" (Washington, DC: NEA, 2012), https://www.arts.gov/sites/default/files/highlights-from-2012-sppa-revised-oct-2015.pdf.

6. "Public Library Use," Tools, Publications and Resources, American Library Association, last modified October 2015, accessed March 23, 2017, http://www.ala.org/tools/libfactsheets/alalibraryfactsheet06.

7. Kathryn Zickuhr, Lee Rainie, Kristen Purcell, and Maeve Duggan, *How Americans Value Public Libraries in Their Communities, Pew Research Center* (Philadelphia: The Pew Charitable Trusts, 2012).

8. "Interview with Lauren Click of the Bronx Museum of the Arts," telephone interview by author, February 25, 2017.

9. Danielle Linzer and Mary Ellen Munley, *Room to Rise: The Lasting Impact of Intensive Teen Programs in Art Museums* (New York: Whitney Museum of American Art, 2015), http://whitney.org/file_columns/0009/7558/room-to-rise.pdf.

10. Gail Dexter Lord, Ngaire Blankenberg, and Richard L. Florida, *Cities, Museums and Soft Power* (Washington, DC: American Alliance of Museums Press, 2016).

11. Nina Simon, *Art of Relevance* (Museum 2.0, 2016).

# 11

# It's Time to Stop and Ask "Why?"

*Lisa Sasaki*

I grew up going to museums where no one looked like me. All those years ago, my story and my family's story didn't fit into the standard narrative of American history and culture. I didn't see people who looked like me working behind admissions desks or behind the scenes. No one I knew worked as a curator, a museum director, or an artist with work in an exhibition. This was not just because I'm Asian American or because I grew up in Wheat Ridge, Colorado (although that certainly contributed to it). I can name many others who did not see themselves in museums back when I was growing up: women, LGBTQ people, Latinx, Blacks, Muslims, Buddhists. . . . The list goes on and on.

What I didn't know then, but I learned once I joined the museum field as a young professional in the late 1990s, is that American museums have had a long-standing diversity and inclusion problem. In 1992, the American Association of Museums (AAM, now the American Alliance of Museums) published its landmark report *Excellence and Equity: Education and the Public Dimension of Museums*. Authors Bonnie Pitman and Ellen Hirzy reiterated concerns about the cultural, racial, and gender imbalance in museums and articulated the need for museums to be inclusive places that welcomed diverse audiences, reflecting America's pluralism in every aspect of their operations and programs.[1] Since then, AAM has reissued multiple—virtually unchanged—editions of this report, challenging museums in each new decade to fulfill their purpose as vital and relevant institutions in service to a diverse society.

Yet since the report was first published, the field continues to struggle with significantly diversifying its audiences, staff, and leadership. Standing in museums and museum conferences today, I realize that my current worries are a perfect echo of Lonnie Bunch's concerns twenty years ago when he wrote his article "Flies in the Buttermilk: Museums, Diversity, and the Will to Change":

I confess, I'm worried. Worried because after more than 20 years in the field, I am still hearing some of the same debates and conversations. Worried because I cannot fully answer the question of why, with so many people of talent and color in this country, more of them are not running our major institutions, leading our curatorial departments, and shaping our educational agendas. Worried because after two decades, I am still "so tired of being alone."[2]

In my worry and aloneness—in my case, being one of the 0.7 percent Asian American museum directors in our field and the 16 percent non-White curators, conservators, educators, and leaders—I have spent a lot of time thinking about why collectively the field has not made greater strides forward.[3,4] This decades-long struggle for diversity, equity, accessibility, and inclusion (DEAI) is not solely due to the continued inaction of museums where these values are still not considered important or valid; there are, in fact, numerous examples of organizations, large and small, who have tested and launched diversity and inclusion efforts. I believe, however, that the ongoing lack of diversity within our museums rests in the complexity and difficulty of challenging deeply engrained beliefs, discussing personal and organizational values, and shifting organizational culture.

Modern management theorist Peter Drucker is attributed with the famous quote "Culture eats strategy for breakfast" along with the theory that organizational culture will inevitably thwart the creation or enforcement of any strategy that is incompatible with that culture. Attempting to increase the diversity of programs, staff, and leadership through tactics and strategies rather than fundamentally altering a museum's foundations—its assumptions, values, vision, and culture—means that long-lasting change does not have the opportunity to take hold. While museums have focused for decades on creating programs for underserved audiences across a full spectrum of demographics, abilities, and identities, museums must now challenge, change, and be held publicly accountable for their organizational cultures, structures, and policies to significantly move the field forward in DEAI.

## MAKING THE CASE FOR A DIFFERENT TYPE OF CHANGE

Since the publication of *Excellence and Equity*, multiple reports have starkly outlined the lack of institutional diversity, most recently the 2015 *Andrew W. Mellon Foundation Art Museum Staff Demographic Report* and AAM's *Museum Board Leadership 2017: A National Report*. Other articles have stated the moral, financial, and demographic imperative to build diverse and inclusive museums. Still others, like the Association of Art Museum Directors' (AAMD) *Next Practices in Diversity and Inclusion*, list the wide-ranging programs that museums are undertaking to increase DEAI in their organizations, but often without looking at their long-term or sustainable impact. Simply put, for the past twenty-five years these reports have stated the problem, emphasized the urgency in which it needs to be addressed, and offered statements on how museums should change (i.e., hire more diverse staff at all levels, provide internal programs on the value of cultural diversity, listen to communities and involve them in decision-making, etc.). But still, after twenty-five years with a clear "to do" list first outlined in *Excellence and Equity*, why have museums failed to achieve the goal of matching America's rapidly growing diversity in their audiences, staff, and leadership?

After summarizing and examining the combined results of these efforts, Gretchen Jennings and Joanne Jones-Rizzi in their article "Museums, White Privilege, and Diversity: A Systemic Perspective," asked a vitally important question—What are we missing?—and suggested that "the roots of our field's persistent lack of diversity and that underlie its challenges in attracting diverse visitors" is this:

1. We focus too much on trying to change others instead of ourselves.
2. Our leadership systems do not consistently serve as models for inclusiveness.
3. The lack of a truly diverse and inclusive leadership in our associations as a whole—a leadership that has examined and rejected the white privilege and oppression that are at the heart of the museum field—contributes to a lack of vision and efficacy in leading the field to embodied diversity and inclusion.[5]

The authors note that most initiatives focus on outside audiences, but little has been done to create internal, systemic change. With education the focus of many museums' missions, it is not surprising that organizations have first concentrated on adjusting their service to and impact on underserved audiences. Take for example AAMD's *Next Practices in Diversity and Inclusion*: Of the fifty-one program submissions from its membership, "exploring a wide range of ways that art museums are striving to become more diverse and inclusive places, both inside and out," only two programs were designated as internally focused with the other forty-nine programs serving a range of individuals including children, college students, families, and community members.[6]

Even as we draw DEAI inspiration from these examples and others in science, history, cultural, and children's museums, I feel that additional questions should be asked, as a professional who led these programs for multiple museums:

• Do the staff who lead these programs feel that the programs are recognized as a vital part of the organization?
• Are the staff who lead these programs supported across the institution or are they "lone warriors," the only people tasked to serve this community?
• Do the audiences served by these programs see themselves in other programs and exhibitions, including permanent exhibitions and collections?
• Do these programs lead to a sustained increase in visitors, staff, and leadership from those underserved groups?
• Have these programs changed "business as usual" for the museum?
• Has the museum found ways to sustain program resources or is the project subsidized through grants and funding that will eventually go away?

I posed these questions not to criticize any particular program, but rather to help us recognize that diversity and inclusion through programs become increasingly difficult to sustain with each "no" or "we don't know" response given. To change noes to yeses—or to change diversity and inclusion programs from prototype or experiment into accepted organizational practice—requires internal, organizational change.

## STARTING WITH YOUR ORGANIZATIONAL WHY

Audience-facing programs were a logical place for museums to start their DEAI work. It was an actionable, immediate, and nonthreatening way (especially with ample grants and funding available to support this type of work) to tackle what could be an overwhelming challenge for institutions. However, the staff who launched these endeavors—often newly hired professionals of color and/or emerging museum professionals—found themselves and their programs on isolated islands within an organization, frequently marooned without adequate resources, staffing, or support. They were asked to constantly justify their projects, educate their colleagues on the need for engaging communities, serve as the sole advocate—and sometimes the organizational watchdog—for these communities, and quietly shut their projects down when funding ran out. After surviving this environment, indifferent at times and hostile at worst, many dedicated professionals chose to move on to other types of organizations and work. Although publicly lauded for their programs, what these staff members seek, on a personal and professional level, is the internal support of their museum and leaders.

To give that support, museum leaders must face hard questions. And answering *why* your museum embraces DEAI—or doesn't—is much harder than answering *how* your institution is exploring DEAI. The museum field has always tried to approach DEAI logically, as demonstrated by the numerous reports and articles stating the business, moral, and historic cases for DEAI produced over the past twenty-five-plus years. While individuals may agree with the data and conclusions, we each also hold competing values and attitudes about ourselves, the world, and other people that have been created through our own experiences. "Why" questions bring these competing values and attitudes to the surface, and they force us to explain ourselves. They complicate something we assumed was simple, expose where we have made assumptions, and often bring people into conflict over differing opinions. Here are a few examples of some challenging DEAI "why" questions:

- Why does (or doesn't) diversity, equity, access, and/or inclusion reflect your organizational values?
- Why does your museum want to work with a specific community (and why not others)?
- Why should diverse individuals work in (or in the case of the board members, volunteer for) your museum?

- Why should (or shouldn't) DEAI efforts be funded at the same level as other museum functions, like collections care or exhibitions?

To avoid the messiness and frustration of answering "why," we skip over this step, not realizing that by doing so we leave those conflicts unresolved, biases unchallenged, and future paths ambiguous. Simon Sinek's management book *Start with Why: How Great Leaders Inspire Everyone to Take Action* outlines simply the danger of leaving our organizational "whys" unanswered: "People don't buy WHAT you do, they buy WHY you do it, so it follows that if you don't know WHY you do WHAT you do, how will anyone else?"[7]

AAM's *Facing Change: Insights from the American Alliance of Museums' Diversity, Equity, Accessibility and Inclusion Working Group* challenges museum leaders to confront this collective blind spot: "Inclusive leadership requires a careful and continuous examination of our implicit biases, which are the often-unexamined tendencies and preferences that we all harbor."[8] The DEAI Working Group's definition of equity—the fair and just treatment of all members of a community—not only acknowledges that equity should be the ultimate goal of our DEAI work, but it also further highlights the need for intentional commitment rather than assuming DEAI will just happen: "[Equity] requires deliberate attention to more than matters of recruitment, hiring, compensation, promotion and retention. Equity includes governance, representation, and other indicators of power. . . . It requires that we deliberately apply time, resources, and consideration in order to achieve this goal."[9] Simply put, we need to better understand the purpose of DEAI, beyond the superficial "it's the right thing to do" or "we need more visitors," and how it can help to transform our organizations.

"Why" questions challenge, but if we take the time to wrestle with them—ideally during staff/leadership retreats with the assistance of a skilled facilitator—the answers can also inspire staff and leadership, prioritize activities, focus messaging, and attract like-minded staff, donors, and funders. Because if we can keep digging to find the common "why" of DEAI within an organization, what you typically discover is a belief statement. Take for example the Oakland Museum of California's (OMCA) value statement about diversity, which OMCA states is fundamental to their institutional culture and guides their collective work: "We believe everyone should feel welcome and part of our community, both within the Museum and with our visitors and neighbors." This statement can be found not only on OMCA's website but also at the top of every job description.[10] According to OMCA's deputy director Kelly McKinley, OMCA is "guided by the belief that when museums are truly welcoming and inclusive, they make a real difference in the lives of people as well as in the health and vitality of a community."[11] This belief led the organization to fundamentally reexamine their mission, vision, management, finances, and programs over a seven-year period, a process that involved staff, board, and community. They have also been able to weather the discomfort and ambiguity that their evolution has evoked:

Lori Fogarty, our CEO . . . often gets asked the question, "So are you a museum or a community center?" and her response is "both." Which is an uncomfortable place to be in sometimes. Some people might feel left behind in the conversation about the inherent value of our collection of objects and expertise, and others might feel we're not going far enough to make change in our community. We're learning to live in a state of discomfort while we find the balance that's right for us, in our city, with our capabilities and resources.[12]

## LIVING YOUR DEAI VALUES

When we address our beliefs on why DEAI should be an integral part of our organizations, we encounter organization culture. The Society for Human Resource Management (SHRM) defines organizational culture as "shared beliefs and values established by leaders and then communicated and reinforced through various methods, ultimately shaping employee perceptions, behaviors and understanding."[13] These shared beliefs create clarity and direction for staff, but only if we are able to articulate them; simply saying "diversity" is a value or that we believe in diversity is not enough. Sinek offers this helpful hint for developing value statements: "For values or guiding principles to be truly effective they have to be verbs. It's not 'integrity,' it's 'always do the right thing.' It's not 'innovation,' it's 'look at the problem from a different angle.' Articulating our values as verbs gives us a clear idea . . . we have a clear idea of how to act in any situation."[14] The Seattle Art Museum (SAM), for instance, states that their core value of diversity is about recognizing that organizations that embody diversity are stronger and more effective; as a result, SAM "invites and respects many viewpoints and experiences, as we strive to develop and sustain a diverse staff and board and showcase art from the world's diverse cultures."[15] Staff and public alike have a clearer understanding of how diversity manifests at SAM, which may look completely different at another museum.

Our organizational values and beliefs must be more than statements written on a piece of paper. If we truly believe in our DEAI values, they should be publicly posted on our websites and in our annual reports; discussed at all staff meetings and during performance reviews; and announced by our CEOs during media interviews and public talks. We must hold ourselves accountable to living these principles, or we dismantle our credibility and trust with our staff and the public. We must allow others, our diverse staff and public, to hold us accountable when we fail to "walk the walk"; and we must allow others to be a part of making decisions about DEAI. This cycle of accountability forces us to take a continual hard look at our infrastructure, policies, practices, and programs, which can be oppressive, privileged, or simply uninformed. Only then can we become inclusive museums.[16]

## MOVING DEAI FORWARD

The saying goes that the definition of insanity is doing the same thing over and over again and expecting different results. While museums should continue to develop programs for underserved communities, we can no longer see these programs as the only solution for increasing museums' diversity, equity, accessibility, and inclusiveness. Instead, museum leaders should use these programs to examine the core reasons why their organizations are engaged in DEAI efforts. In order to be sustainable and successful, these efforts need to be based in institutional values and embedded into the organizational culture. Without scrutiny from staff and the public, museums continue to lack the accountability to make the major changes necessary to move the dial on DEAI. By investing time, resources, and transparency into tackling the bigger issues, hopefully we can see the same major transformation occur field-wide as we have in the few select institutions who have already started the process.

Personally, I look forward to the time when DEAI is the "given" of every museum, when we no longer need business cases to justify the inclusion of those who are not part of the majority. I look forward to the many new perspectives and stories, debates, and growth that will come from this. And I look forward to a time when that Asian American girl from Wheat Ridge, Colorado, won't be so alone in any museum she walks into. Because my "why"—the reason why I continue to work for DEAI in museums—is that everyone deserves to see himself/herself/themselves in a museum.

## NOTES

1. Bonnie Pitman and Ellen Hirzy, *Excellence and Equity: Education and the Public Dimension of Museums* (Washington, DC: American Association of Museums, 1992).

2. Lonnie Bunch, "Flies in the Buttermilk: Museums, Diversity, and the Will to Change," *Museum News*, July/August 2000.

3. BoardSource, *Museum Board Leadership 2017: A National Report* (Washington, DC: BoardSource, 2017).

4. Roger Schonfeld, Mariët Westermann, and Liam Sweeney, *The Andrew W. Mellon Foundation: Art Museum Demographic Survey* (New York: The Andrew W. Mellon Foundation, 2015).

5. Gretchen Jennings and Joanne Jones-Rizzi, "Museums, White Privilege, and Diversity: A Systemic Perspective," *Dimensions*, Special Edition, 2016.

6. Association of Art Museum Directors, *Next Practices in Diversity and Inclusion* (New York and Washington, DC: Association of Art Museum Directors, 2016).

7. Simon Sinek, *Start with Why: How Great Leaders Inspire Everyone to Take Action* (New York: Penguin Press, 2009).

8. American Alliance of Museums, *Facing Change: Insights from the American Alliance of Museums' Diversity, Equity, Accessibility and Inclusion Working Group* (Arlington, VA: American Alliance of Museums, 2018).

9. Ibid.

10. "Culture + Values," Career Opportunities, Oakland Museum of California, www .museumca.org/careers/omca-culture.

11. Kelly McKinley, "What Is Our Museum's Social Impact? Trying to Understand and Measure How Our Museum Changes Lives in Our Community," Medium, July 10, 2017, https:// medium.com/new-faces-new-spaces/what-is-our-museums-social-impact-62525fe88d16.

12. Ibid.

13. "Understanding and Developing Organizational Culture," Toolkits, Society for Human Resource Management, February 12, 2018, https://www.shrm.org/resourcesandtools/tools-and-samples/toolkits/pages/understandinganddevelopingorganizationalculture.aspx.

14. Sinek, *Start with Why.*

15. "Careers," About SAM, Seattle Art Museum, www.seattleartmuseum.org/about-sam/careers.

16. AAM's *Facing Change: Insights from the American Alliance of Museums' Diversity, Equity, Accessibility and Inclusion Working Group* defines inclusion as "the intentional ongoing effort to ensure that diverse individuals fully participate in all aspects of the work of an organization, including decision-making processes."

# Part 3

## THE NECESSITY AND POWER OF FIRST-PERSON VOICES

# 12

# Much Has Been Taken, but All Is Not Lost

## The Restorative Promise of First-Voice Representation[1]

*Eduardo Díaz*

> Not only has the Latino Curatorial Initiative created the space for Latinas/os, but it has provided support along the way to help us be successful. This recruitment *and retention* [are] crucial for building a diverse workforce of people of color from working class backgrounds.
>
> —Margaret Salazar-Porzio, Curator, Division of Home and Community Life, National Museum of American History

## SCENE FROM *NIGHT AT THE MUSEUM: BATTLE OF THE SMITHSONIAN* (TWENTIETH CENTURY FOX, 2009)

[Several historical figures, presumably represented in Smithsonian collections, surround General George Custer, listening to orders.]

Custer: "Any questions?"

[Sacagawea raises her hand. Custer acknowledges her and attempts to pronounce her name, mumbling unintelligible gibberish.]

Sacagawea: "That is not my name."

Custer: "Sacagemea?"

[Sacagawea shakes her head in disapproval. Befuddled, Custer continues to struggle.]

Custer: "Sa-Sack-in-the-Box?"

[One hand on chin, a previously taxidermized monkey gazes up at Custer in annoyed bemusement. Sacagawea again signals her disapproval.]

Custer: "Sheenko-de-Maayo!"

[Sacagawea closes her eyes in understated, exasperated resignation.]

Custer: "Mission accomplished!"

This scene was a segment of a trailer shown to a group of Smithsonian directors at a 2009 meeting convened by Evelyn Lieberman, former Smithsonian assistant secretary of communications and external affairs, and Smithsonian Enterprises, the institution's for-profit arm. Lieberman and Enterprises staff reported on the impending release of *Night at the Museum: Battle of the Smithsonian*, heralding the licensing-derived financial dividends to be reaped.

Any questions?

I raised my hand and said that as a Chicano I was offended by the screenwriter's nonchalant reference to the Mexican holiday of Cinco de Mayo as a comic ploy and asked if Smithsonian content experts had been consulted in advance to review culturally sensitive material. Lieberman retorted—something about this being a good-natured comedy and it being a profitable deal for the institution. (Evelyn is no longer with us. She vigorously served the Smithsonian for thirteen years, leading the institution out of an occasional controversy and relishing in dishing out unvarnished perspectives. We didn't always agree. I miss her dearly. RIP.)

I should note that, ironically, this meeting was held at the National Museum of the American Indian. In retrospect, I very much regret not challenging the demeaning and stereotyping treatment of the iconic Sacagawea and of Native Peoples. As a Mestizo,[2] I should have known and done better. I failed to moderate my Latino identity and give fuller voice to my own indigeneity. Underlying that failure is a complicated web of historical and cultural precedents and personal choice, but that's another story—*otro cuento*.

In September 2016 Pixar Animation Studios invited me to its Bay Area headquarters to see an early cut of *Coco*. *Día de Muertos* (Mexican Day of the Dead) references are woven into the story, so Pixar thought it best to assemble a diverse group of Mexican and Mexican American "thought leaders" to review and comment. Most of the advisors were leery about how this Disney-owned studio would deal with the pre-Columbian religious and cultural practice that is near and dear to us. No doubt the creators of *Coco* recalled the major dust-up when, in 2013, Disney attempted to trademark Day of the Dead in the run-up to the film's production. Not surprisingly, this remarkably insensitive and unwise move met with instant, vocal community fury. Disney quickly relented, and the filmmakers went back to the drawing board. They also went back to Mexico to experience *Día de Muertos* in autochthonous settings and did other homework on the tradition. Pixar engaged community-savvy consultants to help lead them out of the thicket of controversy, diversity strategist Marcela Davison Avilés and noted cartoonist and social critic Lalo Alcaráz. Pixar also assigned a Mexican American codirector, Adrián Molina, to the project. And, importantly, Mexican Americans assumed other key roles on the film's artistic-creative team, including the composers of the film's theme song, Robert López and Kristen Anderson-López.

Our advisory group dutifully offered critiques, suggestions, and encouragement. I saw another iteration of the film in August 2017, three months before its release, and was pleased with several notable improvements to the overall look, feel, and sound of the film. *Coco* has gone on to critical and box office success nationally and internationally, garnering two Oscars for Best Animated Feature and Best Original Song, "Remember Me." *Coco* also won Best Animated Film from the Golden Globes and British Academy Film Awards, and similar recognition from other industry entities. Importantly, the film shattered box office records in Mexico, *tierra firme* of Day of the Dead.

Would *Coco* have achieved success without Mexican American storytelling, composing, and creative leadership? No. Without embedded, lived cultural sensitivity and pride of authorship the film could have been a disaster, or simply another underperforming film panned for its lack of authenticity and reckless use of stereotypes.

Commercial film studios play important storytelling roles in our culture. Their widely consumed products, purposefully or unwittingly, send value-laden messages forward into an active, voracious market, transactions made even more dynamic by ubiquitous usage of social media. Sometimes these messages are culturally and authentically grounded, but too often they distort through disinformation and stereotype. The societal consequences of misguided cultural missiles are enormous and lasting. I harken back to the impressions that Looney Tunes' Speedy Gonzales left with his high-speed antics and demeaning, accented Eengleesh. Or how about Frito-Lay's infamous Frito Bandito? Fortunately, we don't see much of these characters today, but I dare say their distorting cultural baggage is still with us. Pretty loony all right, but not too funny.

Since its establishment in 1846, the Smithsonian Institution's mission has remained the same—*the increase and diffusion of knowledge*. The Smithsonian is the world's largest museum, education, and research complex, operating nineteen museums, nine research centers, the National Zoo, a record label, and a large summer festival on the National Mall. As the Nation's Museum, the Smithsonian is an important conveyor of information and values. Every year, over thirty million visitors cross the museums' thresholds, attend its Folklife Festival, and wander the National Zoo. Many more millions benefit from online visits and music downloads. Annually, the institution makes room for thousands of college interns and emerging scholars. Most would consider the Smithsonian a national treasure.

What happens, though, when important chapters in the country's history and cultural formation are underexplored, or worse, obscured and ignored? What are the consequences when the contributions of communities of color are diminished within the Nation's Museum? The consequences have been and are grave, tarnishing the luster of this national treasure.

When the National Museum of the American Indian opened its doors on the National Mall in 2004, visitors were finally given the opportunity to understand and appreciate the breadth of Native history and culture. (American Indian's George Gustav Heye Center opened in New York City ten years earlier.) The museum has produced many important exhibitions and public programs over the years, increasing and diffusing first-voice knowledge about this country's and continent's first peoples. I invite readers to visit its newest and one of its most engaging permanent exhibitions, simply titled *Americans*, and an upcoming exhibition at its New York venue exploring indigenous legacies and identities of the Caribbean.

In September 2016, the Smithsonian opened the National Museum of African American History and Culture, still the hottest museum ticket in DC. The museum remains crystal clear in its inclusive mission and purpose—to tell a foundationally American story through an African American lens. The average dwell time at a Smithsonian museum is approximately two hours; at African American History and Culture the average approaches six hours. The reality is that there is so much to learn there, much of it newly contextualized perspectives within the narrative of American history. It's not like you can sashay through presentations and programs that span the Middle Passage to the Charlottesville civil disturbance, covering historical periods and cultural movements that have profoundly impacted us all. The museum's beautiful design and the brilliance of its curators, advisors, and leadership have crafted a riveting experience that should not be missed.

In 1994 the Smithsonian released *Willful Neglect*, a report whose title says it all. *Willful Neglect* detailed the institution's failures in representing the history, culture, and contributions of diverse Latino communities. It was a pretty damning and embarrassing report, one that led to further planning efforts and the creation of the Smithsonian Latino Center twenty-one years ago. Over the years, the center has sponsored many exhibits, developed numerous public and educational programs, and supported collecting efforts and publications. The establishment has welcomed hundreds of college-bound youngsters and promising scholars and museum professionals and has generally increased Latino presence at the institution. However, missing was a mechanism to ensure permanent first-voice Latino representation in the all-important, gatekeeping curatorial ranks.

In 2010 the Smithsonian established its Latino Curatorial Initiative, an effort launched by then provost Richard Kurin and the Smithsonian Latino Center. The idea was simple—embed Latina and Latino content experts within Smithsonian units to increase the number of research projects, exhibitions, collections, public and educational programs, as well as publications about the Latino experience in this country, and to ensure that these projects were initiated and managed from a first-voice perspective.[3] To date, curators have been placed at the Smithsonian American Art Museum (E. Carmen Ramos is also now the deputy chief curator), National Museum of American History (Margaret Salazar-Porzio and Mireya Loza), National Museum of the American Indian (Antonio Curet), National Portrait Gallery (Taína Caragol), National Museum of African American History and Culture (Ariana Curtis), Center for Folklife and Cultural Heritage (Amalia Córdova is also now chair of research and education), and Cooper Hewitt Smithsonian Design Museum (Christina De León). A Latino collector is now at the Archives of American Art (Josh Franco also holds the position of national collector). The Smithsonian Institution Traveling Exhibition Service has a project director for Latino initiatives (María del Carmen Cossu), and American History is on the verge of hiring a new Latina/o archivist. Additional positions are forthcoming.

Undergirding this curatorial infrastructure is the Latino Initiatives Pool, federal dollars that support position start-ups and the projects initiated by the curatorial cohort. This support allows the Smithsonian units to leverage private dollars and reorganize internally to permanently establish the positions and enable their foundational work.

To date, the Latino Curatorial Initiative has yielded remarkable results. Where before there was a paucity of Latino exhibits at the Smithsonian, there are now several Latino exhibits displayed year-round, and subsequent exhibitions in research and collection phases. One sees more exhibits including Latino content, including artwork, in other planned exhibits. The Latino collection at the Smithsonian American Art Museum has nearly doubled since 2010. Less than 1 percent of the National Portrait Gallery's holdings were Latino; today the needle has moved significantly. Thirty-three new Latino acquisitions have been completed at the Archives of American Art, with five pledges in cue. Important new collections have been added at the National Museum of American History about the contributions of Mexican American winemakers, most former Braceros,[4] in building Napa's prodigious wine industry, about the history of Spanish-language broadcasting, and about the intricate relationship between Latino communities and baseball (an exhibit opens in 2020), to cite but three examples. The Afro-Latino experience is now receiving concentrated focus at the National Museum of African American History and Culture. A traveling exhibit on the life of iconic labor leader Dolores Huerta will begin its trek next year, with other projects in development. Collecting and programming in the digital realm and popular media has been expanded at the Center for Folklife and Cultural Heritage. Most of the curatorial cohort is also busy publishing books and scholarly articles, and some are active as university lecturers. History curator Mireya Loza recently won prestigious acclaim for her 2016 book, *Defiant Braceros: How Migrant Workers Fought for Racial, Sexual, and Political Freedom*. The cohort regularly present at professional conferences and meetings.

Like all successful museum programs—the Latino Curatorial Initiative received the 2018 Diversity, Equity, Accessibility and Inclusion award from the American Alliance of Museums—it continues to evolve. We recognized that to ensure sustained Latino presence within the units, the cohort needed assistance with research, program planning and logistics, and related activities. Accordingly, in 2017, the initiative approved ten new predoctoral and research assistant contracts, including one who will support collecting and project development on the Deferred Action for Childhood Arrivals Program (DACA), and another to support the Smithsonian's newest pan-institutional initiative on women's history in the run-up to the one-hundredth anniversary of women's suffrage.

In 2008, the federal government established a commission to study the creation of a National Museum of the American Latino, which issued its report to Congress and President Obama in 2011, symbolically on Cinco de Mayo. Later that year bipartisan bills were introduced in both houses of Congress to authorize the Smithsonian to study the feasibility of establishing the museum within its system. Per congressional protocol, revised bills have been reintroduced with the installation of each new Congress. To date the legislation has yet to receive a congressional hearing, despite efforts of the Friends of the National Museum of the American Latino, an entity operating out of the Raben Group, a Washington-based lobbying firm.

Noted scholar and culture critic Arlene Dávila, writing in *Culture Works: Space, Value and Mobility Across the Neoliberal Americas* (NYU Press, 2012), analyzes efforts to establish the Latino museum, suggesting that this exercise is essentially about "the politics of value and worth," and lamenting the positioning of Latinos as "a large consumer base or as rentable political constituency." Viewed this way, one can choose to abide by Dávila's intimation that, up to now, the Latino community is, in the eyes of Congress, not valuable or worthy of a museum on the National Mall.

Exacerbating matters is a persistent flaw in the various iterations of the Latino museum legislation, that of the absence of appropriations language. The bills authorize the establishment of a museum, but do not provide specific, direct appropriations to support planning, design, and construction of the new venue. In establishing the National Museum of the American Indian, Congress and the president approved an appropriation totaling 70 percent of soft and hard costs. In the case of the National Museum of African American History and Culture, the federal appropriation came to $250 million, roughly one-half of the design and construction budget. In both cases the federal appropriation was key in leveraging hundreds of millions in private support. There is little doubt that these private dollars would not have materialized without the federal commitment. In the case of the Latino museum, I think it is fair to say that without federal skin in the game private funders will probably not agree to, essentially, foot the bill for the entire project, estimated to be significantly over one-half billion dollars—this besides the widely held observation that the current Congress and president may not be politically disposed to allocating significant funds to a Latino museum project of this scale.

One of the main criticisms of ethnic-specific museums is that they silo the history, culture, and contributions of the community whose experience they seek to represent, and that they let mainstream museums off the hook relative to the representation of, in the Smithsonian case, Native Americans and African Americans. One can argue that if these national museums had historically done much better jobs of incorporating the experiences of these diverse communities into their exhibits, collections, programs, and governance the American Indian and African American museums may not have been necessary. On the other hand, given the foundational nature of the American Indian and African American experiences in forging the American experience, it is not difficult to justify and openly welcome the establishment of these museums.

I think it is important to note that many years of community organizing and political advocacy preceded the establishment of the American Indian and African American museums. In the most recent case of African American History and Culture, it was President George W. Bush who, in 2003, approved legislation establishing the commission that studied the museum's feasibility. The museum opened its doors thirteen years later. While this may seem like a long time, more telling are the decades of African American community advocacy before 2003. When compared with this precedent, the effort to establish a national Latino museum is in its relative infancy. As noted above, the appropriations flaw in the legislation and the current political realities do not portend well for a timely, clear-path enterprise.

If everything goes according to plan the Smithsonian Latino Center will open a Latino Gallery at the National Museum of American History in 2021. The gallery intends to weave, and center, broad and episodic stories of Latino presence within the narrative of American history. The center will work closely with Latina and La-tino curators already embedded at the museum in developing exhibitions as well as presenting correlative public and educational programs. As noted above, the center will persist with efforts to increase the number of Latina and Latino content experts at Smithsonian museums and continue to support their research, exhibition, collecting, public programming, and publishing efforts.

*No hay mal que por bien no venga.* This popular saying in Spanish, essentially, "Each dark cloud has a silver lining," is apropos in contextualizing the Smithsonian's proven multipronged effort to ensure Latino presence at the institution, one rooted in the premise and practice of embedded first-voice representation.

## NOTES

1. Title inspired by "The First and the Forced: Tracing Historical Overlaps in Native and Black America," Tiya Miles, Ph.D., Mary Henrietta Graham Distinguished University Professor, University of Michigan, from talk given at National Museum of the American Indian, February 15, 2018.

2. A person of combined Amerindian and European descent.

3. Latino includes Latina and gender-neutral Latinx.

4. The Bracero Program, 1942–1964, was based on an agreement signed by Mexico and the United States that brought hundreds of thousands of guest workers from Mexico to work in agricultural and other industries.

# 13

# No Longer Hiding in Plain Sight

*William Underwood Eiland*

I dare not tell it in words—not even in these songs.

—Walt Whitman

One could argue that members of the LGBTQ+ community have made such great gains in the last twenty years that their inclusion in museum exhibitions, programming, and research is a foregone conclusion that many would argue could not be further from the truth. For such critics, museums are too often subject to habits and traditions that depend on retro standards and antiquated policies: some museums are so skittish and thin-skinned that they avoid direct outreach to LGBTQ+ audiences, with the word "queer" rarely being uttered by museum staff. Within the LGBTQ+ community, considering the call for a steady, onward march to greater diversity and equity, it is curious that fragmentation within the community militates against a concerted effort. The initialism by which the community is known is an awkward alliance not without tension and acrimony. In fact, recently some GLB folk (gay, lesbian, and bisexual) would like the "T" (transsexual or transgender) and certainly the "Q" (queer) removed from the initializing, believing as they do that "GLB" indicates a sexual orientation while "T" describes a gender identification. Furthermore, some opine that "queer" is a political statement not descriptive of the entire community and not even appropriate when a second "Q" is added or if (when?) the first "Q" takes on the double meaning of "questioning."

As a means of avoiding a longer, almost tortured, and certainly impossible to remember acronym—such as LGBTQQIP2SAA, a Canadian term, where "I" stands for intersex, "P" for polyamorous (elsewhere for pansexual), "2S" for two-spirited or two spirit, "A" for asexual, the second "A" for ally—a convenient, and to be hoped, not insensitive solution to the proliferations of letters has been to add the plus sign (+) to LGBTQ, thus creating an acronym that includes the entire spectrum of the gender-variant and same-sex community.[1]

In common parlance, however, the word "queer" as an adjective is gaining adherents as a means of asserting pride, of reclaiming a word from the past—and too often from the present—meant to signal opprobrium and loathing, and of establishing meaning for all who reject or repudiate a "specific or static sexual and/or gender identity and embrace queer as a broad identifier."[2] As a theory, even as a method of inquiry, queer history is now a recognized academic discipline, queer literature a genre, and queer art (and its history) a recognized addition to both the vocabulary of labels and ephemera at some museums.[3]

There are those who find this brouhaha over nomenclature unattractive, divisive, reckless, and tedious. Without agreeing or disagreeing, I would rather characterize it as "a community developing its distinctive voice," with the attendant bumps and potholes along the way.[4] In this essay, I intend to adopt "LGBTQ+" for practical purposes.

I would argue that the community may have various coalitions, even schisms, within its ranks, but it represents the greater variety of humankind, the widest swath of human experience, a minority population that encompasses all others, that is perforce inclusive. And therefore, I use unapologetically the word "queers," who are, after all, everywhere, in every ethnic group, of every color, of every culture, religion, class, and age. Sexual and gender variation even occurs among nonhuman fauna; likewise, entomologists have recorded same-sex behavior among insects.

When the former president of Iran Mahmoud Ahmadinejad asserted that homosexuality does not exist in Iran, he betrayed more than his ignorance: He, like too many others, refuses to recognize the mosaic of "queerdom," its ubiquity, its profoundly human nature, its variety of being.

Museums should take note; they may not be in accord even on the vocabulary of liberation, but today's queers refuse to hide in plain sight. They expect museums to recognize that they may indeed be minorities within minorities, but they are individuals with diverse interests and various passions. They are not just footnotes in texts on diversity.

Praise for the twenty-first-century museum comes from those who see it as a temple, as an agora, as a safe place; on the other hand, many see museums as neocolonialist, elitist, antidemocratic hoarders of knowledge as well as of objects. Museums cannot afford degrees of diversity, or inclusion for certain groups, exclusion for other groups, or equity as concept rather than practice.[5]

As a site of reflection and inspiration, the queer-friendly museum has special resonance for audiences with various experiences in self-identifying. We learn from others' paths to pride and, through their exhibitions and programming, museums can be spaces for such solidarity. They can also be places for a contemplative respite, havens where judgment is suspended, even scorned where bias, intolerance, prejudice, and bigotry are not welcome; where, for queer folk, no one fears her or his position on the scale of effeminacy or "butchness." In fact, the museum can be not only a locus for shared experiences but for the very act of sharing them, for finding in the lives of LGBTQ+ scientists, archaeologists, sports figures, artists, and fellow museumgoers an antidote to loneliness—and, if not that, then a response to perceived "aloneness," especially disheartening when one also deals with the recurring nightmares of fear and isolation.

Museums still have a long way to go in recognizing structural homophobia and ensuring it is eradicated in programs, among staff (including those in the chains of governance, such as board members), and in the interpretation of objects, movements, and history. Again, museums have a considerable distance to travel on the road to inclusion when wall labels fail to identify queer artists, scientists, historians, or others—when queer meaning in or from or about an object or idea is distorted, even silenced, in favor of a bland heteronormality that patronizes all audiences by obscuring or whitewashing truths perceived as too fearsome or shocking for the hoi polloi.

Another buzzword of the era is "intersectionality," one that museums more and more need to recognize as a valid, if contested, description of the interconnectedness of the marginalized, the excluded, and the different. Using the vocabulary now passing into standard usage—naming discrimination for what it is in order to understand it and avoid it—homophobia joins sexism, classism, ableism, racism, and ageism as an attitude that divides, that is hurtful, and that is inhumane.[6]

In today's politically charged atmosphere, that "A" for "ally" may loom as an important reminder to museums and their staffs of the need for sensitivity and knowledge in making headway on the road to inclusivity. The reaction to the exhibition of 2016–2017, *Art AIDS America*, organized by the Tacoma Art Museum, illustrates how a desire for inclusivity, while resulting in a powerful and sorrowful statement primarily about the male gay community, fell short despite its good intentions. Protestors staged a "die-in" to decry the near-absence of African American artists from the exhibition even though the Centers for Disease Control reports that more than a third of the over six hundred thousand people who have died from AIDS in the United States are black.

While we know from the Mellon Foundation's demographic study of 2015 that African Americans are just 4 percent of all "curators, conservators, educators, and leadership," we do not know that percentage for LGBTQ+ staff members, nor is there a reliable study of their roles in the so-called intellectual leadership of museums nationwide.[7] To their credit, some museum professionals recognize the need for a queer narrative, and slowly but surely, programming is beginning to reflect and expand knowledge of such life truths for a community for whom oppression has been routine, virulent, and condoned by society, church, and government.[8]

If I were foolish or imprudent enough, I would write a manifesto for queer inclusion in the lives of museums.[9] I would urge museums to learn the vocabulary of "queerdom" in order to avoid stereotypes or offense; to resist the tendency to shy away from truths for children as for adults; to investigate LGBTQ+ folk as saints and villains, as geniuses and idiots, as model citizens and miscreants; people who teach, who entertain, who horrify, who inspire. I would remind museums to engage that community in all its diversity, from programs for so-called alternative families to exhibitions devoted to liberation or oppression.

It would be equally important to me that, while avoiding political and impenetrable cant, museums of whatever type—history, natural history, art, science, and all others—collaborate with the LGBTQ+ community as partners in education, as staff, and as board members, donors, funders, and collectors. Museums should educate their audiences on these issues through films, symposia, lectures, and other traditional pedagogical concepts, realizing that we all learn from other museums' successes and failures in advancing inclusion and that we may find novel means of doing so from peers and from literature on the subject. How aware is your museum of its LGBTQ+ audiences, and is it accessible and welcoming to them? Do they consider the museum their own? In paraphrasing Adrienne Rich, in remaining resistant to inclusive practice, does the museum allow the unspoken to become the unspeakable?

Yes, LGBTQ+ folk can marry . . . at least for now. They can adopt children . . . in some places. They can even hold hands in public . . . or go to the bathroom of their choosing . . . in certain areas of certain urban zones in the not-so-united states. Museums should be expected to expand the advances and overcome the setbacks. One word comes to mind when considering how museums and the LGBTQ+ community must work together to end exclusion, to promote equity, to overcome hate: Pulse.[10]

## NOTES

1. Fred Litwin, "Not My Rights Movement," *C2C Journal*, December 12, 2016, http://www.c2cjournal.ca/2016/12/not-my-rights-movement/. Litwin cites an even longer acronym: "LGBTIQCAPGNGFNBA."

2. *See* "About QTM," Queering the Museum Project, accessed April 5, 2018, https://queeringthemuseum.org/about/.

3. For a good example of a less strident, more balanced explanation for using "queer" as a positive identifier, *see* the introductory essay by Clare Barlow, the curator of *Queer British Art, 1861–1967*, and the editor of its attendant catalogue. She quotes the film director Derek Jarman (1942–1994), "For me, to use the word 'queer' is a liberation; it was a word that frightened me, but no longer." Clare Barlow, *Queer British Art, 1861–1967* (London: Tate Publishing, 2017), 12.

4. Ibid.

5. For further enlightening essays on the subject discussed in this essay, *see* Amy K. Levin, ed., *Gender, Sexuality and Museums, A Routledge Reader* (Oxfordshire and New York: Routledge, 2010).

6. The founders of and writers for the *Incluseum* blog are vocal—too committed to agitprop for those who deplore the language—in presenting critical dialogue about gender equity and museums. Cf. "Demographic studies, such as the Mellon Report, are starting to collect and analyze information about gender's intersections with race and class. If more demographic and data-oriented studies give respondents an opportunity to name experiences as informed by their experiences of race, class, gender, sexuality and ability, the field would be highly impacted in its understanding of equity broadly in museums and how to measure successful inclusion. Current research about museum staff does not account well for non-binary gender individuals or make them visible. Without visibility/acknowledgement (and data) how can we

work to address the ways museums reinforce cisgender privilege and the oppression of non-binary gender individuals and transgender people?" "Gender Equity and Museums," *Incluseum* (blog), February 8, 2016, https://incluseum.com/2016/02/08/gender-equity-and-museums/.

7. Roger Schonfeld, Mariët Westermann, and Liam Sweeney, *The Andrew W. Mellon Foundation: Art Museum Demographic Survey* (New York: The Andrew W. Mellon Foundation, 2015).

8. Consider, for instance, the symposium "Queer Exhibitions/Queer Curating" held at Museum Folkwang, Essen, Germany, in May 2017. "Konferenzen und Kooperationen," Museum Folkwang, accessed April 5, 2018, https://www.museum-folkwang.de/de/ueber-uns/forschung/konferenzen-und-kooperationen/konferenzen/queer-exhibitions-queer-curating.html.

9. LGBTQ Alliance, *Welcoming Guideline for Museums* (Arlington, VA: American Alliance of Museums, 2016). Were I so bold, however, I would have the assistance of this important document in the evolution of LGBTQ+ literature. The LGBTQ Alliance is a professional network of the American Alliance of Museums, and, as such, I think of significance for all museums. The document aligns itself with the Accreditation Commission's Standards of Excellence for Museums.

10. Pulse is the name of the gay nightclub in Orlando, Florida, where, on June 12, 2016, a gunman murdered forty-nine people and wounded fifty-three others.

# 14

# The National Museum of the American Indian

## Whence the "Art Object"?

*W. Richard West Jr.*

*This essay is adapted from remarks delivered at the 1995 Association of Art Museum Directors Annual Meeting.*

I want to share two very different anecdotes from my past. The first involves Eugene Thaw, a highly successful and learned New York collector and art dealer, a generous benefactor of the National Museum of the American Indian (NMAI), and at this point a close friend of mine who has an eye for Indian material akin to God's. Some years ago, as he was introducing me to his collection at his home in New Mexico, he held up before both of us an exquisite carved Tsimshian bowl and, with a facial expression that can only be described as rapt, said, "Nothing in the entirety of the Renaissance surpasses this." From the standpoint of the system of aesthetics as we have come to know it in Western art, Gene was entirely correct.

The second anecdote involves my father, a Southern Cheyenne and a studio-trained painter and sculptor for the vast majority of his current eighty-three years. As a young child, he and I were visiting the Philbrook Art Center in Tulsa, Oklahoma, and we chanced upon a Tlingit object in that museum's significant Indian collection not at all dissimilar in artistic quality from the piece I saw many years later with Gene Thaw. My father told me initially of the object's remarkable beauty, including its material, the artisan's technical skill, its color, and its line. Then, with a slight chuckle, he added, "The only problem is—that's not what it really means."

My father's ironic humor references a difference in perception and understanding that is worthy of the attention of all of us in America's museum community. First, I want to describe, speaking perhaps more as a Cheyenne than a museum director, the cultural context that has a dramatic impact on the representation of Indian objects in a museum setting. Second, I want to address the implications of that context for our work at the NMAI—and perhaps to suggest what may be a possible ripple effect in the art museum community.

Let me turn first to a discussion of those fundamental elements of Indian cultural context that I believe have impact on what the National Museum of the American Indian says through objects to its audiences. While it often comes as a considerable shock to those grounded in the traditions of Western art and less familiar with Indian material culture, the object, if anything, was a secondary consideration to the primacy of the ceremonial or ritual process that led to its creation. In other words, despite the remarkable aesthetic qualities of much of the cultural material we created, our purpose, in the end, was not the creation of "art." A former colleague of mine at the NMAI spoke directly to this point when she wrote:

> [T]he Native artist . . . [values] the creation [of art] . . . over the final product. Process speaks to historical or cultural significance because it is testimony to cultural continuity and change. It is the evidence of lost traditions, innovations, preserved cultural knowledge, historic perspective and vision of the future. . . . It takes into account a sort of "spiritual evidence" that is integral to the creative process. The integrity of the creative process is foremost. The object is meaningless without it.

In discussing the presentation and meanings of Indian material in museums, the second important aspect of cultural context is that Native objects, in their most profound and ultimate dimension, really were statements and reflections—and were intended to be so—of collective and communal values as much or more than they were individual creative statements.

My point is the following. As the son of an Indian artist and a modest collector of contemporary Indian art, I always have loved and appreciated our cultural material for its sheer aesthetic qualities. I have watched with pleasure as this material has come increasingly to be valued on the same basis by others outside the Indian community.

In representing and interpreting the material, however, it is not sufficient, in the end, to treat it only as "art," because we miss much in doing so. A person can stand in awe of a Popovi Da ceramic pot for its beauty as "art," but if he does not know the linkage between Popovi Da's worldview and community and his personal creative spirit, the cultural interpretation of the pot is incomplete—and it can be made complete only by honoring the place of that nexus in defining the meaning of the object.

Significantly, many contemporary Indian fine artists view the matter similarly. Rick Hill, an artist, former museum director, and now member of the staff of the National Museum of the American Indian, puts the matter this way:

> The main difference between Indian and non-Indian artists is that we are still community-driven. . . . Art is the cement that binds the Indian people together, uniting us with our ancestors and with generations yet to be born. Through art we can take a look at why language is important, why ritual is important, why land is important.

With his characteristic frankness and edge, contemporary Apache sculptor Bob Haozous, son of the renowned sculptor Allan Houser, and in my view, an always promising and often brilliant artist in his own right, makes the same point regarding the essential nature of Indian objects.

I want to see people participating in my work. That's totally contrary to what we're taught in America—the artist as an individual, the genius. I don't want to see that in my work at all. I'd rather see, at the most, a cultural reflection of being an Apache. I've been fighting those concepts of individualism, uniqueness, and universalism, concepts that are totally contrary to tribalism. Individualism denies a future or a past awareness. You claim it, you own it, but you're not a part of it.

In other words, through the millennia those Indian people we now call "artists" were not so much in the business of producing "art objects" as they were in creating aesthetically remarkable material whose primal importance lay not in the object itself but in the fact that it reflected—indeed, embodied—the processes, ceremonial and ritualistic, that defined the very community culturally.

How do these principles affect our approach to objects at the National Museum of the American Indian? They have everything to do with what I would call our institution's programmatic self-perception and self-image, which derive directly from our mission statement. Our highest obligation, according to that statement, is to represent and interpret for our audiences the Native peoples and cultures of the Western Hemisphere, past, present, and future. The vast collection of objects that we hold are a means to that end, but do not constitute the end itself. Thus, the National Museum of the American Indian ultimately is categorized most aptly as a museum of culture and cultural history rather than as an art museum.

I know that this conceptual framework is museologically jolting to some, and we heard from a few of them in the critics' community when our inaugural exhibitions opened at the NMAI's George Gustav Heye Center in New York City this past fall. With its characteristic penchant for understatement, the *Wall Street Journal* stated, with respect to a label that referenced the need to look behind the object to the voices of its creators:

> A note explains: "The different voices that surround some of the objects speak for them, since they cannot speak for themselves." Nonsense. These objects . . . speak very eloquently for themselves. Ironically . . . items [in the museum shop] are more respectfully displayed than the museum's own artifacts. Grouped by tribal affiliation and medium, they are in well-lit cases . . . with cards listing only the artist's name and nation. The museum's curators would do well to study them.

I want to be somewhat gentler with this critic than she was with us because her motivations, in one sense, are laudable and seemingly kind. Specifically, she is disconcerted and dismayed by parts of our presentation because we declined to represent and interpret the objects exclusively as "art," which, I would venture to guess is, in her mind and in the Western art tradition, the highest compliment we possibly could pay to the material and the most significant meaning it could have. I am the first to applaud the efforts of many art museums in the twentieth century to liberate Indian objects from the sometimes limiting and deadening gaze of anthropology that brooked no quarter for reading or appreciating Indian objects aesthetically. Nowhere was this liberation more courageously or brilliantly accomplished than by Philadelphia Museum of Art director, Anne d'Harnoncourt's remarkable father, Rene, in 1941 in the MOMA's *Indian Art of the United States*, as well as in the MOMA's similarly conceived exhibits presenting African and Oceanic objects, respectively, in 1935 and 1946.

In the end, however, as the director of the National Museum of the American Indian, I return to a fundamental point of departure. If our mission is to represent, to interpret, to explicate those peoples and cultures indigenous to the Western Hemisphere, we do not serve that mission completely by limiting our presentation to the Indian object as art measured by reference to a system of aesthetics that comes to us from Europe. In doing so we would risk the imposition of an alien interpretive construct that ultimately prevents our appreciation of the object based on the very cultural values and knowledge that give it meaning and significance.

The principles I discussed earlier have a second and significant impact on the National Museum of the American Indian's approach to the representation of objects. Specifically, since our goal is to bring to the material meanings and understandings reflective of the cultural values that motivated its creation, we enlist the Native voice directly and systematically in the interpretive process. In her foreword to the catalogue for an inaugural exhibit of ours at the George Gustav Heye Center entitled *All Roads Are Good: Native Voices on Life and Culture*, our assistant director for cultural resources, Clara Sue Kidwell, describes the rationale for this methodology:

> The "roads" of the title represent the varying cultural backgrounds and ways of viewing objects that the selectors brought to the process of choosing. The reasons for their choices do not necessarily reflect the standards of aesthetic or historic value that might inform displays in an anthropology or history museum. Rather, objects become expressions of distinct ways of seeing the world, an entree for the viewer into a different cultural understanding of the collection. Some common themes emerged during the selection process—the nature of the sacred, relationships with the environment, responsibility to the community, for example—but each individual expressed them in a unique way.

In her foreword to another of our inaugural exhibits, Clara Sue went on to discuss the practical potential of this interpretive approach for expanding and layering the meanings we attach to objects in museums:

> [The] different ways of viewing things confer different kinds of validity. A museum endows an object with importance because it represents some kind of cultural value. The object may represent a certain style of craft work, or it may be unique, or it may meet certain aesthetic standards. Museums become arbiters of meaning in the very process of establishing collecting plans and acquiring objects. Indian people who have lived with objects, on the other hand, bring a different perspective to museum collections. The basket may evoke memories of watching a basketmaker at work. A fringed buckskin dress recalls the hypnotic swaying of many fringed garments as dancers move around a circle to the insistent beat of a drum. The blanket draped over a mannequin recalls the weaver at her loom, the bleating of sheep, the pungent smell of dyestuffs simmering in a pot.

I always have been especially pained by the occasional unfortunate comment that confuses this interpretive methodology with late twentieth century reflexive political sop to the Indian community motivated by a spasm of political correctness. When I, as the director of the National Museum of the American Indian, insist on the implementation of this approach, I am talking culture—not politics. My insistence is premised on a recognition, learned while growing up Cheyenne in Oklahoma, that our culture and cultural sensibilities often are fundamentally different from yours, that we bring those values and sensibilities to the material culture we have created and continue to create, and that, as the creators of these objects, we are in a unique position to enrich the Indian exhibition halls of America's museums.

What, in the end, does all the foregoing mean to me? We Plains Indians, as some of you may know, are fond of quests, and that is how I see my life at the institution over which I preside. I have seen—and I believe I understand—the anthropological and art history paradigms that heretofore have driven the interpretation and representation of Indian objects.

For different reasons I have found both lacking. The former, in its somewhat relentless effort to objectify our cultural patrimony on the basis exclusively of science, can deny access to the sheer delight of pure beauty. While the latter, in measuring the object by reference to purely aesthetic standards originating elsewhere, can limit our progress to an understanding of the intrinsic cultural significance of the object.

In my quest I am comfortable that the National Museum of the American Indian is heading in the right direction, but I do not pretend to know, in my museological youth, the precise location of the interpretive paradigm for which I search. By my approximate midcourse calculation, it sits somewhere on the spectrum between what I refer to loosely as "old anthropology" and "old art history," and, ironically, it will incorporate elements of both, while jettisoning other aspects of each. It is a paradigm that will recognize the aesthetic quality of many Indian objects and will allow visitors to approach and appreciate the material on that basis, but it will not pretend that such an approach marks the ultimate significance of the object. It will bring to the object a cultural surround that adds and enriches meaning and understanding beyond the date on which it was created and the materials of which it is made. It will enlist systematically, as the authentic voices they are, the perspectives of Native peoples themselves in this process of interpretive enrichment.

I alluded earlier to the possible ripple effect of these developments even for the art museum community's representation of objects. Where objects originating outside the Western art tradition sit in art museum collections—and here I include at least African, Oceanic, and Asian objects—I believe that much can be gained in representing the object by augmenting the interpretive approach beyond the prescriptions of art history. I see this initiative, not as an unwarranted and threatening departure from the sacrosanct, but instead as an effort that expands what we museums must tell our audiences about these wonderful things called objects.

I will be fascinated, as an interested observer, to see where art museums and art history go over the next several years. I always have appreciated that, prior to the

Renaissance, the basis on which Europeans viewed the meaning and importance of objects was very similar to much of what I have said this morning about the attitudes of people native to this Hemisphere. So who knows? Although art historians have assumed heretofore that the road to art is straight, linear, and ascending, perhaps, in the end, the path of Western art history may prove far more akin to the Cheyenne cosmology—circular and cyclical.

# Part 4

PERSONAL JOURNEYS

# 15

## Disability and Innovation

### The Universal Benefits of Inclusive Design

*Haben Girma*

*This essay was adapted from remarks delivered at the 2017 AAM Annual Meeting.*

My name is Haben Girma. The name "Haben" comes from Eritrea, a small African country. Ethiopia borders to the south, and to the north is the Red Sea. My mother grew up during the war between Eritrea and Ethiopia. There was a lot of violence. A lot of fear spilled into the classrooms. At school, my mother found that stories helped her find peace away from the violence. Stories are powerful. Stories influence the organizations we design, the products we build, and the futures we imagine for ourselves. My mother heard many stories that said, "America is the land of opportunity . . . America is the land of freedom." Inspired by the stories, she journeyed for two weeks, walking from Eritrea to Sudan, spent several months as a refugee in Sudan, and then a refugee organization helped her come to the United States. Several years later, older, wiser, my mother realized geography doesn't create justice. People create justice. Communities create justice. All of us face the choice to accept oppression around us or advocate for justice.

As the daughter of refugees, a black woman, disabled, stories sometimes say my life doesn't matter. I choose to live a story that says my life does matter, and disability, or refugee status, or the color of my skin won't determine my story. We all have the power to create our own stories. For disability, I choose to believe that alternative techniques are equal in value to mainstream techniques. For everything in my life, from reading to public speaking, I've found alternative techniques that allow me to access information in a different way. For example, a lot of people read books with their eyes, print. I found that I can read books through braille, by using my fingers. For walking around I can use a guide dog. Maxine is my guide dog. She's been trained to guide around obstacles. I've also been trained to use a white cane. I salsa dance. I can't hear the music, but I can feel the beat through the people I dance with. These are all alternative techniques.

Many people don't hear these stories, but they're important stories. Many of you, as museum professionals, must make decisions about which stories you highlight. You can help our community by highlighting disability stories, stories that remind us that different ways of doing things are equal in value to mainstream ways of doing things.

In one of my classes at law school, there was a student sitting next to me. She wanted to say hi, but she wasn't sure how. She waved hi, but I couldn't see it. She said, "Hi," and I couldn't hear it. It was our first day of international law class, and she wasn't thinking about international law. She was thinking about how to get my attention. She did the most logical thing for a student. She went onto Facebook and sent me a message saying, "Hi Haben, I'm sitting right next to you." I actually don't check Facebook in class! After class I saw the message, and I reached out to her and explained how I communicate. If she just typed on my keyboard, I'd be able to read her words on a digital braille display.

When people meet me, the first question they ask is usually, "How do you communicate?" The second question they usually ask is, "Have you heard of Helen Keller?" Yes, actually. Helen Keller was an amazing Deafblind woman who lived from 1880 to 1968. She spent her whole life advocating for women's rights and disability rights. Many people reduce the story of Helen Keller to one thing: a woman who succeeded despite her disabilities. Disability never holds anyone back. Disability is never the barrier. The barrier is society and expectations. When Helen was looking for a college to attend, Harvard wouldn't admit her. Back then Harvard only valued men. Helen's disability didn't hold her back. She was brilliant and hardworking. Her gender didn't hold her back. Many women are brilliant and hardworking. It was the community at Harvard that chose to practice exclusion. Helen did go to college. She went to Radcliffe College, right next to Harvard University. Now Radcliffe is part of Harvard University, but back then Harvard chose to deny access to women. Gender or disability don't hold people back. It's society that creates the barriers.

As another example, Helen's community wouldn't allow her to experience marriage. Helen fell in love, secretly got engaged, but her family forcibly prevented her from marrying the person she loved. Helen's disability didn't stop her from feeling love. She wrote extensively about love. Yet her community, her family, created insurmountable obstacles.

All the barriers that exist are created by people, and it's up to all of us to choose to remove these barriers.

When I was in college I asked myself: what can I do to remove barriers in my community? How can I be the change I want to see in the world? I went to Lewis and Clark College. It's a small college in Portland, Oregon. The cafeteria served as a central place for people to hang out and relax between classes.

When you entered the cafeteria, there were large windows along three of the walls, showcasing Portland's rain. Along the fourth wall were food stations. People would enter the cafeteria, browse a print menu, and then go to their station of choice. As a blind person, I couldn't read the menu. My disability wasn't the problem. Disability is never the problem. It was the cafeteria's choice to provide the menu only in print that was the problem. So I went to the manager and I explained, "This menu is inaccessible. Can you provide it in braille or post it online so that I can use a screenreader to access it?" He told me they were very busy and I should stop complaining and be more appreciative. I don't know about you, but if there's chocolate cake at station four and no one tells me . . . I don't feel appreciative. Back then I was a vegetarian. I would go to a random station, get food, find a table, try the food, and there would be an unpleasant surprise. Sometimes I'd wait in line for twenty minutes only to discover they were serving hamburgers. If they just told me, "Station one hamburger, station two tortellini with smoked Gouda cheese," I would know to skip station one and go straight to station two. I can travel around independently. I can use my guide dog, I can use a white cane. I've developed those skills, but I needed the college to provide information in accessible formats. For the first few months I just tolerated the situation. I told myself, "At least I have food." Many people around the world struggle for food.

Who am I to complain? My mother spent ten months as a refugee in Sudan, and I was getting an education in Portland, Oregon. Maybe the manager was right. Maybe I should stop complaining. I talked to my friends about the situation, and they told me it's my choice. It's our choice to accept oppression or advocate for justice. All these small decisions make a difference. Addressing small obstacles helps us build up the skills to tackle bigger barriers. If we want to shatter the glass ceiling, we need to start with the small steps to make our whole community inclusive. I had a dream of being a part of the disability rights movement. I had a dream of becoming a lawyer and making a difference for people with disabilities. I had a dream . . . of eating that chocolate cake.

The Americans with Disabilities Act was passed in 1990. Congress requires places of public accommodation to provide access for people with disabilities. That cafeteria is required by law to ensure that people with disabilities, like myself, have access. After doing my research, I went back to the cafeteria manager. I explained that I was not asking for a favor, I was asking them to comply with the law. After I framed the issue as a civil rights issue he started to take me more seriously. The cafeteria started providing me the menu in accessible formats. Life became delicious.

The following year, another blind student came to the college. He didn't have to fight for access. He had immediate access to the cafeteria menu, and he could make informed food choices. Small things make a huge difference, and when we practice these small things we develop the skills to tackle even greater challenges and help our whole community become more inclusive.

The experience inspired me to go to law school, and in 2010 I entered Harvard Law School. Harvard told me, "We've never had a Deafblind student before," and I told Harvard, "I've never been to Harvard Law School before." We didn't have all the answers, but we pioneered our way using assistive technology and high expectations. It's okay to not have the answer, as long as you try. Try one solution. If that doesn't work, try another solution. In 2013 I graduated, and now work as a civil rights lawyer helping people all over the world.

It all comes down to these small choices. Which stories do we elevate? What do we believe about access and inclusion? These small choices make a huge difference. The dominant story of disability is that of challenge and overcoming. I believe that disability is about opportunities for innovation and growth.

I want to talk about how disability drives innovation and shows that inclusion is a choice. I have a photo where President Obama is standing at a table, typing on a Bluetooth keyboard. I'm standing on the other side of the table reading from a digital braille display. President Obama usually communicates by voice. When I met him, I explained that I am Deafblind and need people to type on the keyboard so I can read their words in braille. President Obama gracefully switched from voicing to typing, so we could communicate, so that I could have access to his words. That's a choice. There are a lot of people who would say, "No, that's different, that's weird." President Obama shows how these small things can make a huge difference.

Disability has been driving innovation for years. I want to share a story of one of the earliest keyboards. Back in 1808, there were two Italian friends, one sighted, one blind. They wanted to send each other letters. Back in 1808, before braille, before computers, letters were usually written by hand, and that's not accessible to someone who's blind. So what could they do to ensure that the blind friend could write letters to her sighted friend? You might think, "Oh, she could dictate the letter, and someone else could write it down," but these letters needed to stay private. They were love letters. So they thought about it, and eventually Turri, the name of the Italian inventor, built one of the first working typewriters. He built this, so that a blind woman would have the ability to write letters independently and privately.

Behind many of the innovations throughout history there was a person with a disability. We rarely hear these stories. Disability drives innovation, and if we have the opportunity and the choice we need to help highlight these stories, so that we all know that one of the benefits of making our communities inclusive is innovation.

All around the world, Deaf communities have been looking at different ways to communicate, and they've developed sign languages. Every community has their own sign language. The dominant one in the United States is American Sign Language. In France, there's French Sign Language. In the United Kingdom, they have a completely different language called British Sign Language, and it makes no sense to me. People with disabilities have developed these forms of communication. Deafblind individuals hold a hand over another person's hand to feel the signs. When I'm signing with someone, I can feel the signs to access that information.

Another form of communication is dance. There are a lot of communities that try to deny access and say, "That's impossible, that's difficult." However, I was fortunate to find teachers who understood that dance is physical, and there are physical ways to access dance. So through the people I dance with I'm able to access the music and connect with different communities.

Museums are great spaces to explore all the different ways we can communicate information. Touch is a powerful form of communicating information. There is a museum in Madrid, Museo Tiflológico (Museum for the Blind), that has a tactile sculpture of the Eiffel Tower. When I was twenty-two years old, I went to Madrid on vacation, and I learned what the Eiffel Tower feels like for the first time. All my life I'd heard about it, but often it's only portrayed in pictures, in movies. Not until I visited Museo Tiflológico did I actually feel what it feels like.

I'd love to see more museums providing information in physical formats. This is your choice. You have the power to elevate more stories. When you highlight information in multiple formats—touch, visual, audio—you share stories with even more populations. People with disabilities are the largest minority group. In the United States there are 57 million people with disabilities. Around the world it's 1.3 billion people. So you reach more people when you highlight disability stories.

Digital information also needs to be accessible. Digital information starts out as ones and zeroes, and you can choose to present information in visual, audio, or tactile formats. Blind individuals access digital formats through screenreaders. A screenreader is a program that converts graphical information to speech or digital braille. When you program your digital services to be compatible with screenreaders, more people can access them. We're not asking for a separate website or an app for blind people. Separate is never equal. We want one mainstream service that everyone can use. Tell your web or app developers to follow the Web Content Accessibility Guidelines, and Android and Apple mobile accessibility guidelines.

When you make your services accessible, it's easier for disabled and nondisabled people to find your services. You increase content discovery. The Deaf community uses captions. Captions are text that appears on-screen to provide access to audio content on videos. When you add captions to videos, more text is associated with the videos. When you add image descriptions to your photos online, more text is associated with those photos. When people search for keywords it becomes easier to find your product, your exhibit descriptions, and online services.

By highlighting stories of disability driving innovation, you encourage other organizations to choose inclusion. Museums influence society. Spotlighting disability stories may even spark the creation of new accessibility features in the future.

More importantly, by being accessible you meet your legal requirements. Museums are places of public accommodation under the Americans with Disabilities Act, so please do make your spaces accessible to people with disabilities. Our whole community would benefit from museums choosing to elevate and spotlight the hidden stories of people with disabilities driving innovation.

# 16

## Maybe This Time

### A Personal Journey toward Racial Equity in Museums[1]

*Elaine Heumann Gurian*

> True "diversity" means that the visitor of color would need to feel that their very presence did not constitute the diversity.[2]

I have thought of myself as a person with a good soul wanting museums to be relevant centers of internal equity and welcoming to all. For nearly forty years, my writing has come from that consistent philosophical position.

When I began writing in the 1980s, during the Civil Rights era and while on the staff of the liberal experimental Boston Children's Museum, I naively believed that museums were run by those who wanted equity and would be inspired to act toward its achievement. Helpfully, I thought, I produced prescriptive essays. As time went on, I became disappointed that overall change was so slow despite many demonstration projects around the globe led by directors of courage. I then wrote more philosophically about a moral imperative for change. I hoped that leaders would become attracted to some of the ideas. And actually most museum people were interested, some to share, add to, and emulate—but most to avoid.

In the middle of the last century, laws enacted by the U.S. Congress and decisions passed down by the courts began to make segregation and discrimination illegal in different areas of life (i.e., 1947 prohibited real estate segregated covenants; 1954 banned segregation in schools; 1964 repealed the poll tax to suppress poor Black voters; in 1964 the Civil Rights Act was signed that prohibited discrimination based on race, color, religion, or national origin in schools, public facilities, voting, and hiring).[3] And change has come in those listed areas, albeit slowly. At the same time, those who remain unalterably opposed have fought politically to reverse these laws and have become increasingly successful in doing so, bit by bit. Sluggish progress followed by some regression!

The civil rights laws have remained silent about museums specifically, but these legal remedies pertain to museums generically if they are in the federal system or receive federal monies. But such critical national laws set new parameters generally, and museums have been affected by these expectations. Given that national direction, not surprisingly a steady stream of museum staff and writers have called for museums to tackle equity and inclusion for a long time, but with little institution-wide long-term change to show for it. Museum activists have often pointed out that we must include people of color on our boards, our staffs, in our collections, and in our exhibition choices because the American citizenry will soon be majority minority. They have agreed that we will have a declining attendance unless something is done, and if growing a larger attendance is desired, it will have to come from a more varied population.

The additional arguments for supporting the diversification of the workforce have been based on notions of good practice—inclusion of all members of society is ethical and having a workforce of multiple experiences and opinions brings creativity to problem-solving.[4] Why, then, one would ask, haven't museums generally changed their behavior and become broadly inclusive? It must be that the validity of the argument does not build motivation for action.

Here is my list of possible reasons for lack of change:

- Most museums operate with the belief that they are doing sufficiently important good work as is.
- The current audience of "High Propensity Users" (affluent, highly educated, and mostly White) is the basis on which museums plan the present and future. The audience most desired is simply more of the current one.[5]
- There is confusion between class and race, assuming that poor and color are the same. So outreach programs to the poor are deceptively deemed to be sufficient.
- Education attainment and affluence are the two highest predictors of museum use, and therefore the most significant variables are outside the museum's control.
- The act of "welcome" is a culturally dependent endeavor. Museums assume that their normative etiquette is generalizable and universal. Without intentionally including more than one cultural norm, there is no inclusive welcome provided.[6]
- Admission fees and the admissions desk act both as a signifier of and enforcer for including only the desired current audience, not only because in some cases the cost itself is so extravagantly high, but also because the process itself often feels judgmentally exclusionary.
- Museums' existence is used by marketers and recruiting companies to entice wealthy folks to consider moving into the location. Museums are often portrayed as adding desirably to an upscale way of life.
- Museum use is tied to the social approbation of the striving who wish to emulate the mores of the entrenched.
- The content of exhibitions and collections does not seem relevant to segments of society that do not find "themselves" represented, and when they do the group feels patronized because the focus is episodic and targeted.

Museums in America have not remained entirely static. There has been some change. There are more museums with culturally specific programs staffed by people of color. Yet few people of color hold museum-specific jobs of curator, director, etc., when the position is based on general content. Museums overall have a slightly better diversity record when hiring people with transferable skills from outside the museum sector. Jobs in areas such as marketing, security, and finance are somewhat more equitably filled. But shamefully the greatest diversity can be seen at the lowest end of the pay scale such as housekeeping, usually without a career ladder for advancement.

Why hasn't change been ubiquitous, given past grants explicitly based on community building (Lila Wallace Foundation, etc.) or the writing of a more inclusive federal agency policy under Presidents Kennedy and then Clinton? Over the years, when money has been made available toward accomplishing these goals, progress has been made, and when the money ran out, the museums often reverted to their former state.[7] Available funding seems to provide only a temporary motivation. The Mellon Report on Diversity in Hiring in Art Museums makes it clear there is little permanent progress overall to show for these efforts.[8]

## YOUNG ACTIVISTS

Now, in response to the brutality of the killing of unarmed Black men by police in various cities, Americans generally have discovered that parts of their justice system are broken. And these multiple terrible dramatic events have energized young people of color in all fields to assess, and then demand, that change be made now. Activist movements responding to "Black Lives Matter" have appeared in a swath of different civic institutions. The museum community is one such sector.

One must be grateful to young museum professionals of color and their allies who are rightfully calling out the museum community and all who work in it.[9] And they are using the techniques and language of political activism long missing from the American museum scene.

## WORD CHOICE, LANGUAGE, ETC.

These new activists use descriptor words to describe their relationship to the museum world, which I find surprising and harsh. One of the critical current activist dialogues going on in museums is a "Convening on Museums and Race" held in Chicago in early 2016 and continuing in ongoing blogs. A group of professionals with good will and a multiplicity of experiences and backgrounds have carefully written their statement of purpose, which begins:

We believe that it is the persistent and pervasive presence of structural racism in our institutions that are at the heart of the museum field's failure to diversify its boards, staffs, collections, members, and visitors, despite over a generation of effort in this area.[10]

Words are embedded in their (and others') blogs, like systemic, entrenched, or structural racism, oppression, white privilege, white fragility, racial avoidance, intersectionality, microaggression, and reparations.[11,12] These are new words for me. I spend time looking them up and trying to integrate them in my head. I am trying to fit myself into this universe.

Why do the words take me aback? Because I think these are more heated than I have heard before, and words like this I believe describe situations where people's lives are in danger, where government laws need overturning, where lack of supervision causes real harm to people. These words appropriately call the majorities' attention to a failure of safety for others. I think to myself, "Museums in that context are not essential. Symbolic though they are, and centers that can create emblematically, and even real, civic harmony, they are not places where lives are in danger." And so I am chewing over words that heighten the rhetoric.

But in using these words, is not the new activist taking museums seriously, and in ways that I have long wished for? Don't they make it clear that museums, as a coveted bauble of the rich and powerful, might be central to the racist narrative? And museums, in not being truly, profoundly welcoming, only make it worse for those brave citizens who are trying to bring equity to more dangerous areas of public safety. Because of the words that starkly call my colleagues and me out, I find I am taking my sector and its responsibilities in the public arena more seriously. My new journey is because of these words.

I first had to parse the difference between "Black Lives Matter" and my immediate knee-jerk response "All Lives Matter." After study, I have had to agree that "All Lives Matter" is a linguistic trick, used to cover lack of change on the one hand and disguise overt racism on the other. The "All Lives Matter" misstatement begins this winter's internal journey, and I start to understand that one should not hear "Black lives matter MORE" but "Black lives matter TOO."[13] Additionally, I must agree that in the world of frontline law enforcement, where many unarmed Black men have falsely been presumed dangerous and guilty, Black lives have not mattered enough!

My initial misunderstanding of "All Lives Matter" illuminates the way we, in museums, have failed at creating equity in our administrative and programmatic departments. Our rhetoric most often welcomes "all," and in doing so, we are only welcoming more of ourselves. We have not understood that the lives of the culturally different matter TOO and to be equitable, we must now recognize cultural specificity, integrate power-sharing, and incorporate the desires of each community. We must accept that the charge of "structural racism" must lead to structural change. The word and concept "all" is a cover for restating our own norms with the expectation that our standards are universal. They are not!

I conclude that perhaps all museums need to review their mission statements in light of the distinction between "Black" and "All Lives Matter." Upon reviewing many, I find that museums are indeed trying to be inclusive and careful in the stewardship of their objects, but in many ways, are still assuming homogeneity of their visitors.

I, for one, having long written about incremental, and I hoped, achievable change, am without a plan. Understanding that agitation can heighten the call to action but does not cause change by itself, I do not know where the next step is, and I am flummoxed. I am personally not for violent revolution in "Museumland." I am for new administrative rules of engagement and control that mirror social justice. But I do not know what they are, where they are being invented, nor what to advocate for. I have looked at new types of organizational structures in the technology industry and did not think they apply very well.[14]

## POWER

My "good work" is no longer a cover. Uncomfortably, having spent a lifetime trying to make museums welcoming to all, I think I may have got some things right, but at the same time, I may have missed the primary plot. I may be part of the problem, but I sure as hell want to become part of the solution.

I am persuaded that the institutional concept of the collecting museum itself is now, and always has been, intentionally exclusionary. Lack of inclusion is structural and centrally embedded in the museum concept itself. The change needed is not incremental or the imposition of an overlay of a new practice; it is much more thorough-going and central than I have ever considered before.

> Coming to recognize and understand entrenched racism is a difficult and potentially contentious undertaking—but also a necessary step in challenging and transforming the institutional policies and systems that perpetuate structural racism and oppression in museums.[15]

I recognize that, historically, museums, in all forms, are the creation of the powerful, whoever they are. And museums, most especially collecting museums of "treasures," are almost always allied with the ruling structure of the society they are embedded in. In supporting the influential class, museums take on the same goals, aesthetics, enemies, and values as those in authority in their town/city/state/country.

Depending on the museum's locale, power can be in the hands of hereditary monarchs, successful politicians, billionaires, or totalitarian conquerors. The museum per se does not always exclude the same category of people nor is the power always in similar hands. For the museums under Nazi Germany, for example, the specificity of privilege and racism would have been different, the exclusionary policies harsher and more overt, but the system of collusion and social engineering would have been the same. Museums of status, especially art museums, I sadly conclude, are almost always built to transfer concepts of good, worth, and beauty from those in control to those who are not. And these museums tend to garner the most emulation from the museum community itself.

It has always fascinated me that in countries where political revolution has occurred, and independence over colonialism or occupying nations has become the law of the land, the new powers have elected to create their museums quite like institutions of their persecutors. And emerging countries with new wealth have built traditional but modern museums to assert that they too are powerful. When formerly marginalized people in the United States create a museum of their own, their first iteration is often a reproduction of the museums of their oppressors. Experimentation and customization often await the second or third installation. They want, they tell me, to be taken "seriously," and that seemingly requires imitating the powerful.

That museums are the handmaidens of the wealthy and influential has been recognized for a long time. Many scholars have said this for decades.[16,17,18,19] I have read the material eagerly, have cited many to bolster my arguments. I now believe that until we change the structural power arrangement—embedded in the concept of collections and knowledge ownership—describing the problem and asserting the ethical imperative will not bring about change. Reluctantly, I admit I am, however else I might define myself, part of the establishment.

## AMERICAN MUSEUMS

Private not-for-profit American museums, because of their reliance on the largesse of people with access to funds, have an interwoven collaboration between the board, funders, and staff. It is a familiar arrangement for publicly displaying once privately held objects for the edification of the have-nots. Fundamentally, those in control believe the values of the museum and their role in it do not need an overhaul. They do not consider their museum a flawed institution. Quite the contrary, they believe that museums are an act of public service and therefore good. They are accordingly immune to the argument for change.

The naming of buildings and exhibition spaces gives rise to the distortion this intertwined relationship can bring. The naming of David Koch exhibition rooms in both the American and National Museum of Natural History for a donor, part of whose wealth is based on energy, and who funds climate deniers and lobbies against effective climate legislation, is one such example. This same closed-loop relationship can be seen in art museums as they attempt to navigate the problematic relationship between their funders who are collectors, exhibition choice, and the art marketplace.

Interestingly, government museums, which could create different governance structures, mimic the private museums in their desire to have people of wealth on their boards. They have government relations staff whose job it is to appeal to elected officials in the same kind of complicit equation as with the rich. In fact, government museums seem more susceptible to those in power; witness the "Enola Gay" controversy when the Smithsonian canceled a proposed exhibition to mollify the congressionally upset.

Perhaps equity will be more visible in museums when, and if, the results of the presidential elections change. In the future when the voters will include a more active minority electorate, museums might become more equitable in response to governmental granting agencies that will demand it. However, for the time being, activity in this sector seems retrograde.

## PERMISSIBLE CHANGE

Overall the American museum is not entirely immune to change. Boards of directors may agree that museums could use some tweaking, given changing demographics, but they do not envision fundamental reassessment. Boards, given their fiduciary obligations, will remain fundamentally protective of their funders' interests and status. What they will continue to look for is upper-class people of color.

Understanding that the audience of middle-class highly educated "White folk" is a declining base from which to work, museums have often stated the necessity to broaden the visitor base and have created programs to attract others. These are typically based on assuming that those of color and other excluded peoples will aspire to be associated with the same cultural conventions that govern now. The fantasy goes: the new visitor, most especially the hoped-for middle class of color, will see the value of museums as currently constituted and will eagerly enter. That may be a false assumption, or it may be true that class trumps culture. If diversity of visitors and opinion is really wished for, then issues of class will finally have to be dealt with.

The most profound change is that museums now take audiences more seriously and treat them more carefully than when I began. Museum staff study and adopt best practices in customer services, which they mimic from the commercial sector. For those in charge, however, there is a hope that when hiring workforce members of color, the new staff will replicate the white team in education and etiquette. The new personnel will "pass" if you will. And the powerful will show off the newly hired as examples of the museum's diversity, but at heart, nothing fundamental will have changed. Instead, I conclude that resistance to broad-based inclusion is intentional, successful, and even quasi-pious. Further, many staff members act as guardians at the gate sent to protect against what they perceive as assaults by wrong-headed liberals on their precious objects, their accompanying knowledge, and their access to the rich—just as their predecessors did before them.

## CHANGE AGENT DIRECTORS

But while social justice, as now conceived, has not been historically central to the formulation of museums, let us recognize that throughout history there have been directors who sought otherwise. When equity has been achieved, it is because the director and their colleagues intend it to be so and they revamp the organization's fundamental guidelines and align themselves with others who believe the same. Their work is often widely known by almost everyone in the field. But alas, their work does not cause system-wide change because, I now think, the work is considered exciting but aberrant. When individual personality, vision, and empathy lead the way, assisted by a band of the committed staff, they are the shooting stars . . . not the solid firmament.

## NOT WHITE

Why am I taking this so personally? Maybe because as James Heaton writes in his blog Tronvig Group:

> I'm going to talk about race. This means, if you are white, I have probably already activated in you something called racial anxiety—a fear of what I am going to say, and probably also a strong desire to run away.[20]

But most likely, I am unnerved because I have never thought of myself as White before. I am a Jew, and therefore have unswervingly thought of myself as non-White and subject to constant, if subtle, alienation. To those who wanted to put me in the White category, I have said: "If the world wants to treat me as White then, and only then, will I check the White box. Until then I remain 'other.'"

I have carried my Jewishness as a proud emblem putting me in a tribal category where I can better align with indigenous people and people of color. I have prized the opportunity to work with museums dealing with the explicit story of formerly excluded people, of official museums of "very bad news," and with national museums deciding that the disenfranchised should have their stories told.

Given that context, I believed I could work with vigor on issues of cultural equity and be on the right side of justice. I dismissed that appalling fact that some people in my own category of Jewishness have been found to be flagrant racists, repeating the actions against others that had been used unjustly against us.

While being Jewish is not one of the specific official U.S. Census categories of otherness and never has been, in working on my family genealogy there is plenty of evidence that officials used it at immigration centers and on census forms as an important descriptor. So while I do not count in the official record-keeping categories, I belong to a group in which discrimination is clearly known.

There are other groups of peoples included in the non-overt alienated categories in the United States. I remember when Italians and Irish were not "White" and when it was legal to refuse to hire them, and segregated housing could state explicitly that no Blacks, Jews, Catholics, or Irish need apply. Now Muslims, in overtly insulting language, have joined the evolving list of permissible shunning.

Yet to own up to my experience, those in the unofficially excluded group get some, maybe most, but not all, of "White Privilege." In part, because economic advantage trumps culture when it comes to entree and I am rich enough, thanks to the hard work of my father and the real estate training he gave me. And given the list of advantages to be found in papers like "Unpacking White Privilege," it is clear that I have assumed as much privilege as possible whenever possible.[21] And I train my children and grandchildren to do the same. I teach each one to enter every Ritz-Carlton Hotel, or the like, with an air of invincibility as a way to navigate the city's toilet facilities, and it works all the time because they are well-dressed and look white.

Yet I understand that in 1986, when I was a candidate for director of the Boston Children's Museum where I had worked for sixteen years, I was asked questions and endured comments (like "how can I take you to my banker?") that I could have used to bring discriminatory charges, but didn't. I know that there exists in my land, formerly overt, now covert, Jewish quotas for college entrance, bank loans, and country club admissions. It was not legal and when uncovered, sheepishly changed. But it is so systemic and long-lived that Wikipedia has an entry titled "Jewish Quotas."[22]

## BECOMING WHITE

Yet despite the privileges I have enjoyed, even though I never feel "White," I now must move to the side of the powerful to take responsibility. Nikhil Trivedi says, "When we benefit from power we have privilege, when we are dominated by power we are targets of oppression."[23]

At the Museums and Race convening held in Chicago in 2016, an unnamed museum professional said:

> There is an urgent need for white museum professionals to address their privilege and role in oppressive systems. People of color bear a large burden when their white colleagues expect them to raise their awareness of racism and oppression.[24]

Elinor Savage, a program officer at the Jerome Foundation, has explained it this way in a public lecture on October 26, 2015:

> For white people who define as anti-racist, we can't position ourselves as separate from covertly and overtly racist people. We have to be responsible and accountable for shifting the paradigm of racism. We have to create space for anti-racist learning that is not punitive. This work has to come from a place of love and compassion.[25]

It is, belatedly, clear to me that our colleagues of color cannot be left to change the museum world alone. Advocating for change is also my responsibility. But having always supported reform, what is different now is more fundamental and central. What is different now is that I cannot choose the terms nor control the outcome.

I am about to become a foot soldier (an ally) in someone else's army. I am not currently in the "love and compassion" place, but understand I need to work toward it.

## HOW WILL CHANGE HAPPEN?

I am thrilled, in principle, to see these new activists requiring that we pay attention and finally bring systemic change. But I feel old, out of touch, irrelevant, and guilty. We did not get this done when we should have. But "maybe this time," I say to myself. As Elinor Savage said in her brilliant speech:

> We are living in a historic moment. A once-in-a-generation moment in which we have again reached a crisis point in dealing nationally with crucial issues of race. And we seem doomed to repeat again and again if we do not stand up to the challenge of transforming ourselves.[26]

Once again, we have a collective chance to change museums into institutions that work for all, make all welcome, and forget no one. Maybe this time, we will make systemic change. But how? Reluctantly, I no longer think that "standing up" alone will bring about change, because those that control the system are not interested. I have concluded that change will need to be imposed externally. Disruption does get people's attention, but better still there needs to be new legislation, guidelines for funding opportunities, a legal suit under new or possibly existing labor laws, and voting for parties and specific candidates committed to social equity. When elected officials are beholden to voting blocks of color and their allies, maybe then their agencies will become more interested in fairness and this will have a contagion effect.

The Native American Graves Protection and Repatriation Act (NAGPRA) stands as the most central alteration of museum practice in my work life, and that was forced by legislation in the U.S. Congress.[27] No amount of agitation by native tribes and goodwill caused wide-scale voluntary compliance in the United States. Only laws imposed and the penalty for failure started the process, though foot-dragging has been the compliance record. The law changed only when Indigenous people had more voting and economic power than previously, when casinos gave them real money to affect elections, and when they could file suits that won in the courts. NAGPRA happened as well when some brave White museum directors agitated through the government rather than with their peers to get this done.

For those who don't like this imposed solution, there is a chance that change may come through stealth. Perhaps diversifying hiring practice will bring change internally and more organically.

More staff of color may indeed bring about more cultural change in collection acquisition, topic choice, collections care, exhibition methods, and attendance one museum at a time. And that is, partly, the motivation of those who are arguing for more people of color within each museum.

Many museums have a stated commitment to acting as agents of social change, but we see an inconsistency between this mission and museums' internal labor practices. We believe that only once museums recognize and resolve their internal inequalities can they truly begin to act as agents of social change.[28]

Since the employment of people of color in museums remains stubbornly underrepresentative, what will cause new hiring outcomes now—if not legal imposition—I do not know.

A museum director friend suggested that diversifying the collections also has a stealth effect. The new collections remain embedded in the museum for the long term and need care and research that brings them to the fore. The museum with new, more representative objects will become more responsive from the inside out, the argument goes. I am skeptical, because I have seen many places where objects of the minority have been mislabeled, presented out of context, or left to molder. Nevertheless, I add this as an area to contemplate.

## CONCLUSION

My big takeaway is this: advocating voluntary change is manifestly unpersuasive for those players holding power in museums. For racial change specifically, and social justice generally, there will have to be legal sticks and/or financial carrots. Given episodic but unsustained funding by foundations now and in the past, permanent change in museums will likely come only when enforced from the outside, enhanced by the presence or imminence of a minority majority.

My journey continues. My pledge to help the young, committed museum workers of color, who bring much-needed energy, is unabated. I am determined to focus on new avenues when they are presented. I hope that real change will come this time. But in my older age, I am not optimistic that I will see it in my lifetime.

## NOTES

1. In 2016, I wrote this paper in Vieques, Puerto Rico, where I live in the winter and where I do most of my writing. At the time, I had a different topic in mind that I was researching, but the world of the Internet and the emails of my colleagues kept intruding and disturbing my focus. I was highly influenced by and dedicated to the members of the Museum Group who responded to and then helped to cause the "Convening on Museums and Race." I was fearful about this endeavor and shouldn't have been. I began to use their bibliography and the blog of the convening as my lessons, having daily interrogated myself on a journey from righteousness toward uncertainty and discomfort. At the end of the winter I wrote to myself: "I leave Vieques with a paper of a journey with no surety that it will be delivered or has any worth but writing it allowed me to organize my thoughts at least for now." I sent the paper at the time to Laura Lott, the CEO of AAM, because we occasionally exchange written thoughts and trust each other. To my surprise she kept the writing and two years later asked me to

consider allowing it to be published. So here it is, a publication of a personal journey by someone who uses writing as a way of thinking.

2. Porchia Moore, "The Danger of the 'D' Word: Museums and Diversity," *Incluseum* (blog), January 20, 2014, http://incluseum.com/2014/01/20/the-danger-of-the-d-word -museums-and-diversity/.

3. Selected from a list of federal civil rights laws found in Wikipedia. Wikipedia, "United States federal civil rights legislation," last modified September 17, 2017, https://en.wikipedia .org/wiki/Category:United_States_federal_civil_rights_legislation.

4. David A. Thomas and Robin J. Ely, "Making Differences Matter: A New Paradigm for Managing Diversity," *Harvard Business Review* (September–October 1996): 70–91.

5. Colleen Dilenschneider, "High Propensity Visitors: The True Attributes of People Attending Museums and Cultural Centers," Know Your Own Bone, October 23, 2013, http://colleendilen.com/2013/10/23/high-propensity-visitors-the-true-attributes-of-people -attending-museums-and-cultural-centers-data/ (article was removed from website by August 6, 2018).

6. Elaine Heumann Gurian, "Intentional Civility," *Curator: The Museum Journal* 57, no. 4 (2014): 473–84, https://doi.org/ 10.1111/cura.12086.

7. "YouthALIVE! Program," Wallace Foundation, accessed March 20, 2016, http://www .wallacefoundation.org/learn-about-wallace/GrantsPrograms/our-initiatives/Past-Initiatives/ Pages/Youth-Alive.aspx (page was removed from website by August 6, 2018).

8. Roger Schonfeld, Mariët Westermann, and Liam Sweeney, *The Andrew W. Mellon Foundation: Art Museum Demographic Survey* (New York: Andrew W. Mellon Foundation, 2015).

9. MuseumWorkersSpeak, *How Do We Turn the Social Justice Lens Inward? A Conversation about Internal Museum Labor Practices*, AAM 2015 "Rogue Session" (n.p.: MuseumWorkers-Speak, 2015), accessed March 22, 2016, https://drive.google.com/file/d/0B3UU5M-r8dW 7M3Jac2d6NmZXcFk/view.

10. The Museum Group and the American Alliance of Museums (convening, *Museums and Race: Transformation and Justice*, Chicago, IL, 2016).

11. Porchia Moore, "The Danger of the 'D' Word: Museums and Diversity," *Incluseum* (blog), January 20, 2014, http://incluseum.com/2014/01/20/the-danger-of-the-d-word -museums-and-diversity/.

12. Nikhil Trivedi, "Oppression: A Museum Primer," *Incluseum* (blog), February 4, 2015, http://incluseum.com/2015/02/04/oppression-a-museum-primer/.

13. Harvey Simon, "Black Lives Matter Too," *Huffington Post*, October 19, 2015, http:// www.huffingtonpost.com/harvey-simon/black-lives-matter-too_b_8316882.html.

14. M. Cossentino, S. Galland, N. Gaud, V. Hilaire, and A. Koukam, "How to Control Emergence of Behaviours in a Holarchy" (conference paper, Second IEEE International Conference on Self-Adaptive and Self-Organizing Systems Workshops, Isola di San Servolo, Venice, October 20–24, 2008), https://doi.org/10.1109/sasow.2008.28.

15. The Museum Group and AAM (convening, 2016).

16. Michel Foucault, *The Order of Things: An Archaeology of the Human Sciences* (New York: Vintage Books, 1973).

17. Pierre Bourdieu, *Distinction: A Social Critique of the Judgement of Taste* (Cambridge, MA: Harvard University Press, 1989).

18. Jürgen Habermas, *The Structural Transformation of the Public Sphere: An Inquiry into a Category of Bourgeois Society*, trans. Thomas Burger with Frederick Lawrence (Cambridge, MA: MIT Press, 1991).

19. Tony Bennett, *The Birth of the Museum: History, Theory, Politics, Culture: Policies and Politics* (London and New York: Routledge, 1995).

20. James Heaton, "Museums and Race," Tronvig Group, accessed February 26, 2016, http://www.tronviggroup.com/museums-and-race/.

21. Peggy McIntosh, "White Privilege: Unpacking the Invisible Knapsack," *Independent School* (Winter 1990).

22. Wikipedia, "United States federal civil rights."

23. Trivedi, "Oppression."

24. The Museum Group and AAM (convening, 2016).

25. Elinor Savage, "A Call to Action," Arts in a Changing America, accessed February 19, 2016, http://artsinachangingamerica.org/2016/02/09/a-call-to-action/ (article was removed from website by August 6, 2018).

26. Ibid.

27. Native American Graves Protection and Repatriation Act of 1990, 25 U.S.C. 3001 et seq.

28. MuseumWorkersSpeak, AAM 2015 "Rogue Session."

# 17

# Museum Musings

## Inclusion Then and Now

*Cecile Shellman*

I sit near a window, writing this article during a particularly snowy spring in western Pennsylvania, recalling some of the most significant moments of my life and career. On my next birthday I will have lived two score and ten years, celebrating a milestone built with memories spanning countries and states, relationships and roles. It will also mark twenty-five years in the field of museums, working in or closely with almost every traditional department there is: education, marketing and communications, human resources, operations, curatorial, and exhibitions. It's hard to pick a favorite role.

As I hold my lanyard stretched taut, looking down at my current work badge, I read the title "Diversity Catalyst" and smile. My charge, as a catalyst among four museums in a complex system in Pittsburgh, Pennsylvania, is to direct and oversee diversity, inclusion, and accessibility efforts internally and externally, institute-wide. Compliance to regulations, training others in cultural competence, and fostering inclusive environments are key hallmarks of the position. It's an executive-level position in a one-thousand-plus-person organization and is one of just a few of its kind in museums in the United States. This job didn't exist, wouldn't have existed twenty-five years ago. So much has happened since then: to the field, to me, to this country, and to the world. As I write and reminisce, I can point to several pivotal moments, people, readings, and memories that have effected internal, external, and field-wide change to this end.

I've fulfilled at least one of my childhood dreams: to work in museums. As a young person I was fixated with material culture; I was fascinated by objects and the stories that made them come alive. I was born and raised in Jamaica, a Caribbean island of, at the time, a population just over two million people. It is an old island but a young country, having gained independence from Great Britain less than a decade before I was born. Its motto, "Out of many, one people," mirrors the United States' similar affirmative stance, just as its history of conquest, enslavement, oppression, independence, and struggle are similar. I'm descended from enslaved Africans who were brought to the Western Hemisphere as part of the Middle Passage. I'm also descended from some who were the persecutors and colonizers—it's all wrapped in one confusing, concerning package. Like most in the West Indies, Brazil, and other countries where the transatlantic slave trade forced high numbers of enslaved people to take the place of *farm implements* and *household appliances* in a most ignominious manner, I struggle to reconcile my genealogical heritage.

I've never wanted to be anything other than who I am, but I recognize that blackness is fraught with negative assumptions reinforced by (White) Western civilization's cultural biases.

It was hard enough living with that realization as a child and as a teenager in a majority-black culture, but moving to Idaho in the 1980s demonstrated what it means to live in a majority-white space. Even today—at least at the 2010 Census, the state of Idaho is only 0.6 percent black or African American. It's painful to recall some of the questions I was asked by either curious or hostile peers and adults on a regular basis. That said, I found comfort, solace, and lifetime friendship among those who were decent and kind.

I attended college at Brigham Young University in Provo, Utah, where I was one of about six black students on campus. In a large private university of more than thirty thousand students, this was shockingly significant. Most of the others were male athletes, including a certain 6'8" basketball player—almost two feet taller than me—whom others would try to link romantically to me, since we just "belonged together." The school, and the religion that sponsored it, was engaged in efforts of inclusivity much later than many other similar organizations. This meant that I was often a trailblazer or pioneer for many activities and programs that were meant to foster multiculturalism. I spoke in front of groups; shared songs, food, and stories; encouraged questions; and patiently gave answers. It was exhausting and sometimes discouraging, but it needed to be done and there were few of us to do it.

By the time I worked as a museum store supervisor and later as education curator at the Museum of Church History and Art in Salt Lake City in the mid-late '90s, I was well used to a lack of diversity in business environments where race, ethnicity, and religion were concerned. At the same time, training dozens of docents and volunteers who were retirees allowed me to challenge my own prior assumptions about age and disability. Sometime during my tenure there, I came across the *Excellence and Equity: Education and the Public Dimension of Museums* article from a 1992 publication. I was intrigued. The article resonated with me on a profound level. I had never before come across a reading that acknowledged and even nudged professionals towards introspection for the purpose of increasing diversity or being inclusive. This was huge. The article was written for educators but was potentially useful to others in the field. Authored by a team of passionate and dedicated museum administrators organized as the American Association of Museums Task Force on Museum Education, the paper made an emphatic case for seeking multiple perspectives in planning and decision making; having diverse representation among leaders and visitors alike as a basic standard of museum operation; and taking active, affirmative steps to develop standards and best practices in inclusive behavior.

Many of the concepts expounded in *Excellence and Equity*—in particular those heralding openness, respect for all, and collaborative problem-solving—were already evident in my work at that particular museum, but I was beginning to see that it was not necessarily so field-wide. I also had no opportunity to test, and no true feeling for, the racial and ethnic issues at the museum. Besides occasional visits by my own family of origin or visiting friends, it was incredibly rare to see a black visitor at that institution. I had a coworker who didn't know what to call me; when I left my employment there he shyly remarked that he was glad to know me, as he had never interacted with a "dark person" before.

Branching out regionally and nationally proved helpful. I soon joined what was then the American Association of Museums (now the American Alliance of Museums) and started attending conferences. I don't remember putting two and two together: despite how impressed I was by the 1992 article, I either forgot or didn't understand that the piece was commissioned by that very organization. In fact, it was hard to see that, given that the membership was, on its face, not very diverse in terms of race, ethnicity, or socioeconomics as far as one could tell. While it was great to be surrounded by "my (museum) people," who experienced similar joys and frustrations around museum work, the same gnawing, empty feeling would visit when I realized than in these spaces, too, I was one of not too many; I was the "other."

By the year 2000 I was living in Boston, Massachusetts, intent on completing a graduate course of study at Harvard Extension School. The graduate certificate program, a precursor to the University's ALB in museum studies, was among a smattering of comprehensive museology programs in the United States. I was a mature student, already having worked as a museum professional, but returning to acquire credentials that I never knew I needed.

There didn't seem to be many museology graduate programs back then. No one I knew—not at the museum for which I'd worked, nor among my friends who had college degrees in art or art history—had attended such a thing. Museum practitioners at the Museum of Church History and Art came from various trades and disciplines: academia, woodworking, fine art, elementary school teaching. Each staff member applied specific skills and knowledge to the work at hand. We worked collaboratively; we sought each other's counsel and camaraderie.

Mostly, I was excited to move to a region of the United States that was more cosmopolitan, more ethnically diverse, and more densely populated than the Intermountain West was with people of African descent. I was ready for a change of scenery, and to see how museums operated in other cities. I had learned to love Salt Lake City, but it was not known for its diversity or inclusion. It still suited me better than other towns in which I'd lived in Utah, however: towns where the Sunday school kids would shyly brush up against me and ask if I was made of chocolate. I envisioned New England, and Boston in particular, to be a place where museums told the stories of more than one people, where the visitors represented a variety of ethnicities, and where other voices and views were better respected.

The East Coast, which I'd only visited briefly previously, was a cosmopolitan delight. As with Temple Square, there were people from all countries, backgrounds, and ethnicities—but they also lived there, working, eating, deriving their living and satisfaction from being around each other. I had not experienced this on such a scale in my life, and it was quite fascinating to me.

It was soon after I arrived in 2000 that Dr. Lonnie Bunch's article "Museums, Diversity, and the Will to Change" was published in the July/August edition of *Museum News*. Not only did I feel vindicated in my decision to pursue the museum studies course of study, I felt that on reading this my cohort and others would take counsel and comfort in a person of color's take on museums for the future. I had never read an article by a person of color, that I knew of, about museum matters.

The article confirmed much of what I had observed for myself on both sides of the country as a resident, and throughout the United States as a visitor or tourist: Where were the African American or African-descended museum employees? Beyond curators and administrators at culturally specific institutions, where were the other professionals? Where were the students of color?

In my own coursework, and among my diverse, but international, classmates and friends I would pose these questions. Many of the international students wanted or needed additional museum certification outside of professional degrees and work. There were students from Italy, Greece, and Turkey. Those students planned on returning to their home countries once they graduated. As far as Africans or African-descended scholars and classmates were concerned, however, I was alone. Another young woman had signed up for the program and not returned to complete the course.

New England is a museum aficionada's playground. From the mighty Museum of Fine Arts Boston to any number of idyllic house museums or boutique spaces, there is something for everyone. From sprawling exhaustive collections and blockbuster exhibitions to single-object museums, the opportunity to seek enrichment from museum spaces is pervasive.

In the Museum Studies Department, all the professors and the vast majority of students were White. We visited all the Boston museums and then some for coursework, and I did not run into many people of color there either. If I did, they were likely to be nonprofessional staff, working in generic service roles such as cafeteria workers or security guards. I was reliving my Utah experience in a city that was ostensibly much more diverse. How and why was this happening?

*Dangerous Curves: The Art of the Guitar*, a blockbuster exhibition that was displayed at the Museum of Fine Arts Boston in 2000, was lavish, sumptuous, and engaging. It spoke equally to lovers of the lyric and casual listeners as it did to seasoned practitioners; to crafters and makers of fine instruments to historians hailing supposed historical European roots of the instrument. Noticeably absent, however, were any mentions of the instrument's likely West African roots. Where were the *balafon*, the *goje*, the *krar harp*? Even the *sitar* from India is an early form of the guitar. Many of these instruments were invented and played hundreds of years before Europe was settled. Yet *Dangerous Curves* only featured the European story. It was shocking, yet somehow not surprising.

In November, the same month of the blockbuster's premiere, another *Museum News* article was published, this one by Carlos Tortolero, founding director of the Mexican Fine Arts Center. Like Bunch, Tortolero lamented the assumption that mainstream museums were already inclusive, when this is and was hardly the case. (See "Museums, Racism, and the Inclusiveness Chasm," 2000.)

Back then, matters of access and equity seemed to reside in the province of the museum education department or the development department; sometimes both. The museum educators cared about reaching out to the "underserved," and the development departments wanted to demonstrate that the museum was truly compassionate by way of its outreach to children. But what I finally learned, through these articles and my experiences to date, was that museum diversity and inclusion work is not the same as museum outreach.

I interned, and later worked full-time, for the John F. Kennedy Presidential Library on beautiful Columbia Point in an I. M. Pei–designed building in Boston. I barely knew then, but I know and appreciate deeply now, how remarkable an institution this is and was, in the service of civic action and human rights. After the horror of 9/11, I was asked by then–education director Tom Putnam to develop a program that brought school students together and affirmed concepts of pluralism. Even further, staff at this museum openly and explicitly acknowledged the role of jingoism, nationalism, racism, and racial profiling in contributing to societal ills. I was proud to help create an award-winning long-term program called *Dialogues on Diversity*. Students from various parts of Massachusetts convened at the museum to meet and learn from each other in respectful discursive exercises. Tonya Lewis Lee's beautiful documentary about race, *I Sit Where I Want*, was shown to many of these groups as part of the exercise. A partnership with the Consensus Building Institute yielded thoughtful curriculum that engaged and challenged student and museum educators alike.

The JFK programs created in response to both the tragedy of terrorist action and community input were profoundly moving—even life-changing. It was at this moment that I truly started to understand how instrumental a museum can be as a convener, collaborator—even healer—when it comes to matters of inclusion.

In subsequent years, through work responsibilities at a number of museum spaces and art institutions in New York, Massachusetts, and Pennsylvania, I have used my experiences at the John F. Kennedy Presidential Library and the living words of these seminal articles referenced earlier to bolster my resolve as I continue to be a champion for museum inclusion and critic of exclusion.

Inclusion is not outreach. It is not an hour of drumming and dancing on Martin Luther King Day. It is more than providing temporary exhibits or transitory programs that feature the "exotic other." Inclusion means making real-life, real-time continued efforts to ensure that all those who previously experienced exclusion at the expense of a powerful majority are now intentionally, fully included.

It takes awareness, consciousness-raising, trust-building, authenticity, and bravery to create lasting equitable change. Acknowledging the role of museums and other long-standing institutions in historic oppression is often difficult for those in leadership roles to believe or accept. Another challenge for museum administrators is embracing the notion that inclusion is not merely one individual's or one department's province or problem.

In the last five to ten years, a remarkable wave of words and voices has made its way through many museum spaces across the nation and the world. Museum workers are speaking up about wage injustice; museum professionals of color are being hired from traditional museum programs; museums themselves are thoroughly evaluating their hiring practices, which are too often informed by bias and apathy.

Organizations that are centered in bettering the museum environment for visitors and employees of color, the LGBTQ community, and others are springing up: groups like Museum HUE, web-based platforms like *Incluseum*, in-person convenings like MASS Action, and others have arisen to inform, educate, and actively pursue the best practices in inclusion.

The American Alliance of Museums itself is truly modeling principles of allyship by embedding inclusion in the latest version of their strategic plan and highlighting equity at their annual and other periodic meetings. The organization's board is now comprised of a significant number of persons of color. AAM leaders are listening to, and learning from, the wisdom of official and grass-roots inclusion experts.

In my current work at Carnegie Museums of Pittsburgh, I am truly fortunate to be able to influence museum practice at the leadership level, while working hand-in-hand with staff and volunteers who may not yet have an authoritative voice. This is accomplished by way of collaborative task force meetings; focus groups; through the work of visiting scholars and friends; workshops on disability justice, communication strategies, and racial diversity; among other strategies. I like to stress that the goal of equity is reached by acknowledging and encouraging diversity, championing inclusion, and creating accessibility. An inclusive approach requires each staff member to internalize and own their part in inclusion efforts. Beyond celebrating multiculturalism, the approach should continue until there is representation and meaningful inclusion at all levels and across all platforms.

I am honored to have met and worked with several second-wave pioneers who echo Dr. Bunch, Dr. Johnnetta Cole, and others who have been stalwarts in the service of inclusive museum practice for decades. When I consider my museum work and life at the very beginning of my career, as opposed to now, I see a remarkable trajectory and feel a profound sense of pride and hope.

# Appendix A

Diversity, Equity, Accessibility, and Inclusion Definitions

# DIVERSITY, EQUITY, ACCESSIBILITY, AND INCLUSION
## DEFINITIONS

### DIVERSITY

Diversity is all the ways that people are different and the same at the individual and group levels. Even when people appear the same, they are different. Organizational diversity requires examining and questioning the makeup of a group to ensure that multiple perspectives are represented.

### EQUITY

Equity is the fair and just treatment of all members of a community. Equity requires commitment to strategic priorities, resources, respect, and civility, as well as ongoing action and assessment of progress toward achieving specified goals.

### ACCESSIBILITY

Accessibility is giving equitable access to everyone along the continuum of human ability and experience. Accessibility encompasses the broader meanings of compliance and refers to how organizations make space for the characteristics that each person brings.

### INCLUSION

Inclusion refers to the intentional, ongoing effort to ensure that diverse individuals fully participate in all aspects of organizational work, including decision-making processes.

It also refers to the ways that diverse participants are valued as respected members of an organization and/or community.

American Alliance of Museums

# Appendix B

The Andrew W. Mellon Foundation Art Museum Staff Demographic Survey

REPORT

# The Andrew W. Mellon Foundation
Art Museum Staff
Demographic Survey

July 28, 2015

*Roger Schonfeld*
*Mariët Westermann*

With *Liam Sweeney*

THE
ANDREW W.
MELLON
FOUNDATION

# INTRODUCTION

In June 2013, the Andrew W. Mellon Foundation made a $2.07 million grant to the Los Angeles County Museum of Art to enable the museum and four other major metropolitan museums in the United States (Art Institute of Chicago, High Museum of Art, Museum of Fine Arts, Houston, and Nelson-Atkins Museum of Art) to launch a pilot program of undergraduate curatorial fellowships.[1] The initiative was designed to open up the museum as a potential workplace to students from historically underrepresented minorities and other undergraduates who are committed to diversifying our cultural organizations. At a time of unprecedented rates of demographic change in the United States, the program was intended as an experiment in what may need to be a concerted effort, supported by many organizations, to make the country's art museums more representative of the growing diversity of the American people. In each of its five sites, the program met with enthusiastic responses, but also with questions. Why was such a program needed? How did the art museums and the Mellon Foundation know that demographic homogeneity was a problem in art museums?

To people familiar with the professional profiles of American art museums or with the graduate programs that prepare students for jobs at the intellectual heart of museums, the questions may seem naïve. Both the relative underrepresentation of people of color on art museum staff and the preponderance of men in museum leadership positions are well known phenomena, subject to regular discussion in the Association of Art Museum Directors (AAMD), American Alliance of Museums (AAM), Association of Art Museum Curators (AAMC), and Center for Curatorial Leadership. Nevertheless, the questions focused the Foundation's attention on the absence of reliable data about the demographic makeup of art museum staff across the country. Aware of AAMD's recent finding of a pronounced gender gap in museum directorships,[2] the Mellon Foundation proposed partnering with AAMD to conduct a demographic survey of art museum staff and boards. In the fall of 2014, the Foundation commissioned Ithaka S+R to design and implement a survey with the assistance of an advisory committee of AAMD staff and member museum leaders. AAM supported the effort by enabling distribution of the survey to art museums that are not AAMD members. In the winter of 2015, 77% of AAMD institutions and 15% of the additional AAM cohort completed the staff survey. AAMD and AAM response rates for board diversity were considerably lower (38% and 4%, respectively), and too unrepresentative for inclusion in this report. While the report below is generally limited to the AAMD respondents, the findings for the smaller AAM group are not substantively different from those for AAMD museums. More than 90% of respondents were in the United States; there are a few institutions from Canada and Mexico in the sample.

The results summarized by Ithaka S+R below lead to a range of conclusions, many of which are perhaps best addressed by museums on the local level, as local and regional demographics tend to differ considerably across the continent. The headline is unsurprising: utilizing the categories employed by the 2000 U.S. Census, 72% of

AAMD staff is Non-Hispanic White, and 28% belongs to historically underrepresented minorities.[3] As the American population is today 62% Non-Hispanic White, the overrepresentation of this group on museum staff may at first not seem as dramatic as one might have expected. Ithaka S+R's analysis shows, however, that there is significant variation in demographic diversity across different types of museum employment. Non-Hispanic White staff continue to dominate the job categories most closely associated with the intellectual and educational mission of museums, including those of curators, conservators, educators, and leadership (from director and chief curator to head of education or conservation). In that subset of positions, 84% is Non-Hispanic White, 6% Asian, 4% Black, 3% Hispanic White, and 3% Two or More Races. With the exception of the Asian demographic category, which makes up 5% of the United States population today, these proportions do not come close to representing the diversity of the American population.

Two specific results point to pathways for diversifying museum leadership and the positions that shape museums as venues of research and lifelong education. First, progress is likely to be swifter and easier on gender equality than on minority representation. As museum staff has become 60% female over the past decade or so, there is now also a preponderance of women in the curatorial, conservation, and educational roles that constitute the pipeline for leadership positions such as museum director, chief curator, and head of conservation or education. With close attention to equitable promotion and hiring practices for senior positions, art museums should be able to achieve greater gender equality in their leadership cohorts within the foreseeable future.

Second, there is no comparable "youth bulge" of staff from historically underrepresented minorities in curatorial, education, or conservation departments. The percentages of staff from underrepresented communities in such positions are basically level at 27.5% across the different age cohorts born from the 1960s to 1990s. Therefore, even promotion protocols that are maximally intentional about the organizational benefits of diversity are not going to make museum leadership cohorts notably more diverse if there is no simultaneous increase in the presence of historically underrepresented minorities on museum staff altogether, and particularly in the professions that drive the museum's programs in collection development, research, exhibitions, and education. This finding suggests that diverse educational pipelines into curatorial, conservation, and other art museum careers are going to be critical if art museums wish to have truly diverse staff and inclusive cultures. It also indicates that the nation will need more programs that encourage students of color to pursue graduate education in preparation for museum positions, such as the AAMD/UNCF diversity initiative and the undergraduate curatorial fellowship program supported by the Mellon Foundation.

While the results of the 2015 art museum staff demographic survey may seem discouraging, they provide baseline data against which future surveys can be measured, and, one hopes, progress tracked. For their energetic and thoughtful collaboration on the survey, the Mellon Foundation is deeply grateful to AAMD President Susan

Taylor and Executive Director Christine Anagnos, former AAM President Ford Bell, Director Elizabeth Merritt of AAM's Center for the Future of Museums, and all the directors and HR directors of the art museums who responded to the survey and reacted to an initial presentation of results at the 2015 AAMD annual meeting in Detroit. Directors of AAMD member institutions lent invaluable advice to the Foundation and to Ithaka S+R; for their time and insights, we thank Gail Andrews, Andrea Barnwell, Johnnetta Cole, Timothy Rub, and Julián Zugazagoitia. At Ithaka S+R, Deanna Marcum, Roger Schonfeld, and Liam Sweeney were tirelessly persistent and thoughtful in the design, administration, and interpretation of the survey.

As a small beginning, the 2015 art museum staff demographic survey lends support to the resolve of the many institutions that seek to mirror the country's demographic transformation and become fully inclusive of the interests of their diverse communities. The case is clear and urgent, and constructive responses to it will be critical to the continued vitality of art museums as public resources for a democratic society.

Mariët Westermann
Vice President
The Andrew W. Mellon Foundation

## METHODOLOGY

Ithaka S+R developed the survey with the advice of AAMD museum leaders and HR directors, AAMD staff, and Mellon Foundation program staff. The questionnaire was split into three components: A spreadsheet that each museum was asked to fill out indicating the demographic categories into which each of its employees fell; a survey questionnaire targeted at HR directors, which focused on museum diversity programs; and a survey questionnaire targeted at museum directors, which focused on board member diversity and policy issues.

In the employee spreadsheet, we gathered demographic and employment information in a variety of categories. We asked respondents to categorize each employee into one of 17 job categories as indicated in Figure 1. We asked respondents to categorize each employee by race and Hispanic/Latino status, and we elected to utilize the U.S. Census categories from 2000 that are used for various reporting purposes, notwithstanding their limitations, as indicated in Figure 2.[5] For analytical purposes, we frequently combine categories to provide binary analysis of the categorizations "White Non Hispanic" and "Historically Underrepresented Minority," abbreviated as "Minority." We asked respondents to categorize each employee by gender, offering the choices of "Male," "Female," and "Does not identify as either male or female." We recognize that all these categorizations collapse a great deal of complexity and diversity but elected to use them for ease of data gathering and analytical comparisons with other existing data sources. Finally, we asked for information on decade of birth and decade of employment.[6]

**Figure 1.  Job Categories**

| Conservators | Curators | Education |
|---|---|---|
| Exhibition Design and Construction (includes Fabrication) | Facilities | Finance/Human Resources |
| Information Technology/ Web Development | Marketing/Public Relations | Membership/Development (includes Event Planning) |
| Museum Leadership (includes "C" positions) | Preparators/Handlers | Publication/Editorial |
| Registrar | Retail and Store | Rights/Reproduction (includes Photography) |
| Security | Support/ Administrator | |

**Figure 2.   Race and Ethnicity Categories**

Race

- White—A person having origins in any of the original peoples of Europe, the Middle East, or North Africa.
- Black or African American—A person having origins in any of the Black racial groups of Africa.
- American Indian or Alaska Native—A person having origins in any of the original peoples of North and South America (including Central America) and who maintains tribal affiliation or community attachment.
- Asian—A person having origins in any of the original peoples of the Far East, Southeast Asia, or the Indian subcontinent including, for example, Cambodia, China, India, Japan, Korea, Malaysia, Pakistan, the Philippine Islands, Thailand, and Vietnam.
- Native Hawaiian or Other Pacific Islander—A person having origins in any of the original peoples of Hawaii, Guam, Samoa, or other Pacific Islands.
- Two or More Races—All persons who identify with more than one of the above five races.

Hispanic or Latino—A person of Cuban, Mexican, Puerto Rican, South or Central American, or other Spanish culture or origin regardless of race.

- Yes
- No

The survey was fielded from February 2, 2015 and was closed on March 13, 2015. Invitation messages were sent to AAMD museums by Mellon vice president Mariët Westermann and AAMD president Susan Taylor, and to other AAM art museums by vice president Westermann and AAM president Ford Bell. Several reminder messages were issued by the same individuals. The message to AAMD members indicated that the survey was mandatory, and AAMD also conducted direct outreach to its members.

Response rates varied between the AAMD and AAM populations, and also by the different survey components, as seen in Figure 3. In this overview report, we focus on AAMD respondents, drawing demographic data from the employee spread-sheets. Those findings are based on a 77% AAMD response rate to that component of the survey.

**Figure 3. Levels of Response**

|  | AAM | | AAMD | |
|---|---|---|---|---|
|  | *Number* | *Percent* | *Number* | *Percent* |
| Total Art Museums | 643 | 100% | 235 | 100% |
| Spreadsheets Returned | 97 | 15% | 181 | 77% |
| HR Surveys Completed | 105 | 16% | 206 | 88% |
| Director Surveys Completed | 27 | 4% | 90 | 38% |

## EXECUTIVE SUMMARY: RACE AND ETHNICITY

- In the aggregate, AAMD museum staff are 72% White Non Hispanic and 28% Minority. Staff composition varies significantly across respondents, ranging from 100% White Non Hispanic to 100% Minority, as illustrated in Figure 4. Many but not all of the museums that are majority Minority are culturally specific institutions. Some but not all of the museums that are 100% white are located in geographical areas that may have comparatively lower Minority populations.

- Many job categories are highly specific to White Non Hispanic employees or, to a lesser extent, to Minority employees. As Figure 5 shows, Security and Facilities staff are split fairly evenly between these two groupings. Other job categories are majority White Non Hispanic, with approximately 9 out of 10 Registrar staff being White Non Hispanic. Figure 6 drills in on a subset of Job Categories that includes Curators, Conservators, Educators, and Leadership (a category that is broader than just the director to include other "C-level" employees), showing that this group is 84% White Non Hispanic, 6% Asian, 4% Black, 3% White Hispanic, and 3% Two or More Races.

- In terms of year of birth, younger employee cohorts appear to be somewhat more diverse. Of employees born in the 1930s, about 20% is minority; this percentage grows to approximately 30 for employees born in the 1980s and 1990s, as shown in Figure 7. In the Job category subset (Figure 8) of Curators, Conservators, Educators, and Leadership, the pattern of apparent change is even more gradual, with percentages hovering around an almost steady 27.5% for Minority employees born in the 1960s, 1970s, 1980s, and 1990s.

- The employees in six job categories that are heavily Minority (Facilities, Security, and Finance/HR) or White Non Hispanic (Leadership, Curators, and Conservators) are 20-30 years older than the majority of museum staff.

**Figure 4. White Non Hispanic and Under Represented Minority, By Museum**

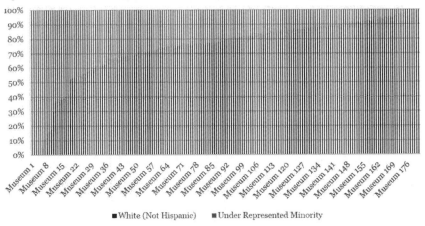

**Figure 5. White Non Hispanic and Under Represented Minority, By Job Category**

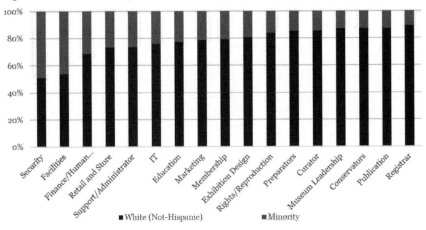

**Figure 6. Race and Ethnicity (Curators, Conservators, Educators and Leadership Only)**

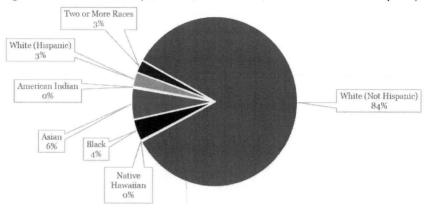

**Figure 7. White Non Hispanic and Under Represented Minority, By Decade of Birth**

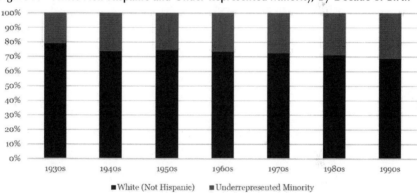

**Figure 8. White Non Hispanic and Under Represented Minority, By Decade Born (Curators, Conservators, Educators and Leadership Only)**

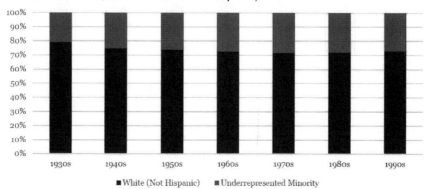

## EXECUTIVE SUMMARY: GENDER

- In the aggregate, AAMD museum staff are 60% Female and 40% Male.[6] There is significant variation among individual museums, varying from 94% Female to 63% Male, as shown in Figure 9.

- Many job categories are highly gender-specific, as shown in Figure 10. Facilities, Preparators/Handlers, Exhibition Design and Construction, IT, and Security are heavily weighted towards Males. Rights/Reproductions and Museum Leadership (again, a category that is broader than just the director to include other "C-level" employees) are each approximately equally staffed by Male and Female employees.[7] Other job categories, including the subset of Curators, Conservators, Educators, and Leadership, are approximately 70% or more Female.

- By decade born, museum employees appear to be growing comparatively more Female, as shown in Figure 11. For the job category subset of Curators, Conservators, Educators and Leadership, Males remain approximately 35-40% of museum staff regardless of decade born, as shown in Figure 12.

These findings show a notable difference between race/ethnicity and gender in terms of the availability of younger professionals to move into leadership positions over time.

**Figure 9. Gender, By Museum**

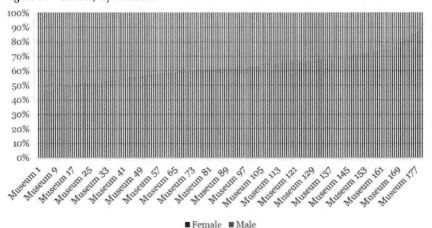

■ Female  ■ Male

**Figure 10.   Gender, By Job Category**

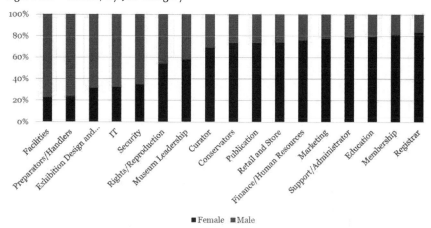

**Figure 11.   Gender, By Decade Born**

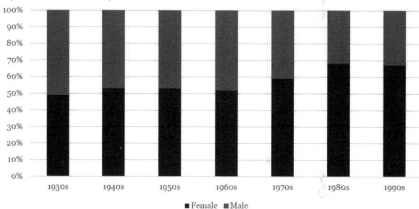

**Figure 12.   Gender, By Decade Born (Curators, Conservators, Educators and Leadership Only)**

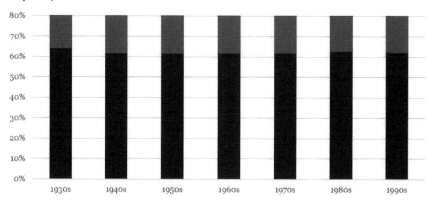

# NOTES

1. http://www.lacma.org/node/13365.

2. Anne-Marie Gan *et al.*, "The Gender Gap in Art Museum Directorships," report of the Association of Art Museum Directors and SMU National Center for Arts Research, March 7, 2014; available at https://aamd.org/sites/default/files/document/The%20Gender%20Gap%20in%20Art%20Museum%20Directorships_0.pdf.

3. For the purposes of producing a baseline picture of the demographic composition of art museum staff in North America, the survey employed the widely used racial and ethnic categories introduced in the 2000 U.S. Census. They are the most convenient tool for measuring diversity, but there is a growing and cogent critique that they do not adequately capture the true diversity of the American population. For an introduction to this problematic, see Kenneth Prewitt, "Fix the Census' Archaic Racial Categories," *New York Times*, August 22, 2013; Prewitt was director of the United States Census Bureau from 1998 to 2000. The categorizations are of even more limited value for institutions in Canada and Mexico.

4. These categories were adopted by the federal government for equal opportunity reporting purposes and therefore are in common use at many institutions in our survey population. For more details, see Source: http://www.eeoc.gov/employers/eeo1survey/2007instructions.cfm.

5. We considered asking about LGBT status and/or disability status but determined that there would be regulatory or legal issues in many states associated with employers tracking or reporting these data to us.

6. Less than 1% identify as neither male nor female, according to the museums completing the spreadsheets. This is likely an underrepresentation of actual identity percentages but reflects the fact that so many employers track this categorization on a binary Male/Female basis.

7. By comparison, AAMD's recent report found that 43% of directors themselves were women, with significant disparities in salary as well; see Gan *et al.*, 2014.

# Appendix C

Museum Board Leadership Report Excerpt—
The People

The success of nonprofits is often measured in terms of social good, and people are at the heart of the nonprofit enterprise. The museum director and board members — together with other staff and volunteers — represent the talent that the organization can draw on to advance the mission and move the organization forward.

If we want high-performing organizations, we must ensure that we have the right people at the helm to provide vision, strategy, oversight, and leadership. This requires different and complementary backgrounds and experiences, judgment, engagement, and ongoing attention to how we fill the leadership seats at the table.

## Demographics At-a-Glance

The following is a snapshot of current board and chief executive demographics, as reported by museum directors:

### FIG P1 — GENDER, AGE, RACE/ETHNICITY[3]

| GENDER | Museums | | | LWI | | |
|---|---|---|---|---|---|---|
| | Director | Chair | Board | CEO | Chair | Board |
| Male | 38% | 62% | 55% | 28% | 58% | 52% |
| Female | 62% | 38% | 45% | 72% | 42% | 48% |
| Other | 0.3% | 0.4% | 0.0% | 0.0% | 0.1% | 0.2% |

| AGE | Director | Chair | Board | CEO | Chair | Board |
|---|---|---|---|---|---|---|
| Less than 40 years old | 12% | 5% | 10% | 11% | 11% | 18% |
| 40 to 49 years old | 19% | 12% | 16% | 20% | 17% | 25% |
| 50 to 64 years old | 51% | 39% | 40% | 57% | 44% | 41% |
| 65 years or older | 19% | 44% | 35% | 13% | 29% | 17% |
| Mean | 54.8 | 60.9 | NA | 53.8 | 56.6 | NA |

| RACE | Director | Chair | Board | CEO | Chair | Board |
|---|---|---|---|---|---|---|
| American Indian or Alaskan Native | 1.0% | 1.3% | 1.4% | 0.4% | 1.0% | 0.9% |
| Asian | 0.7% | 1.1% | 1.9% | 1.5% | 2.2% | 3.0% |
| Black/African American | 2.0% | 3.0% | 5.2% | 4.1% | 4.8% | 7.8% |
| Caucasian | 93.0% | 92.6% | 89.3% | 90.2% | 89.9% | 84.3% |
| Native Hawaiian or Pacific Islander | 0.4% | 0.1% | 0.4% | 0.4% | 0.1% | 0.4% |
| Two or more races | 1.7% | 0.7% | 0.3% | 1.8% | 0.5% | 2.8% |
| Other, please specify | 1.3% | 1.1% | 1.6% | 1.7% | 1.4% | 0.8% |

46% of museum boards are 100% white. 30% of all nonprofit boards are 100% white.

| ETHNICITY | Director | Chair | Board | CEO | Chair | Board |
|---|---|---|---|---|---|---|
| Hispanic or Latino of any race | 3.5% | 2.2% | 3.4% | 2.9% | 3.3% | 4.7% |
| Not Hispanic or Latino | 96.5% | 97.8% | 96.6% | 97.1% | 96.7% | 95.3% |
| Prefer Not to Answer | 45 | 44 | NA | NA | NA | NA |

3 This survey followed the U.S. Bureau of the Census that distinguishes between race and ethnicity. Race categories are White, Black, Asian, Native American/Alaskan Native, Hawaiian, and other Pacific Islander, "some other race," and "more than one race". There are only two ethnicities in the Census classification: Hispanic/Latino, and not Hispanic/Latino. Hispanic people can be any race.

## Diversity and Inclusion

One of the most striking changes in the composition of the United States since 1984 has been the dramatic expansion of the minority population. A fundamental challenge for museums is that while the population is already one-third minority, heading towards majority minority, today only 9% of the core visitors to museums are minorities and approximately 20% of museum employees are minorities. If museums want to be relevant to their communities, they must address these discrepancies.[4]

As leadership teams recognize the need to adapt their organizations to society's changing needs, this includes examining who is sitting around the boardroom table, which is where critical decisions are made. Various backgrounds and experiences (professional and personal, as well as cultural and ethnic) add to the quality of the board. A board is often expected to "represent" the organization's community as a way to create accountability and form a link with the public.

The demographic profile of museum board members reveals considerable ethnic and racial homogeneity along with minimal age diversity. Board composition is tipped to white, older males — more so than at other nonprofit organizations. Forty-six percent **(46%) of museum boards are all white**, compared to 30% of nonprofit boards.

Research suggests that lack of diversity in board composition may be a network problem. Ninety-one percent (91%) of white Americans' social networks are other white Americans, which is the racial group that dominates nonprofit board and chief executive positions.[5] Board members tend to be older and from wealthier populations, and their social networks also tend to be majority white.[6] These factors both explain and perpetuate the problem of board diversity.

Whether hiring the museum director, recruiting board members, allocating resources, or serving the community with authenticity, the board's commitment to diversity, equity, and inclusion matters. The data show that museum directors and board chairs are in agreement that diversity and inclusion are important to help advance their missions, especially when it comes to "understanding the changing environment from a broader perspective," "understanding the museum's visitors," and "enhancing the organization's standing with the general public." Further, 77% of museum directors and 66% of board chairs indicate that expanding racial/ethnic diversity is important or greatly important. Museums fall short, however, when it comes to taking action. According to museum directors, only 10% of boards have developed a plan of action for the board to become more inclusive, and only 21% have modified policies and procedures to be more inclusive.

### WHAT WE FOUND
Of the various diversity categories, museum directors are most dissatisfied with the lack of racial diversity on boards. While 57% of museum directors have agreed that it's important to increase board diversity, only 10% report that the board has developed a detailed plan of action to become more diverse.

64% of museum directors are dissatisfied with the board's racial diversity.

43% of museum directors are dissatisfied with the board's age diversity.

24% of museum directors are dissatisfied with the board's gender diversity.

### WHY IT MATTERS
Museum directors understand that the lack of diversity impacts their ability to advance the mission and meet the needs of their members, yet, like many nonprofits, museums are struggling to adapt their board recruitment practices.

Becoming more diverse requires moving beyond conversation to intentionality. It requires an action plan and the examining of interpersonal dynamics and the cultural fabric of the board and organization. To help move the board forward, consider the following questions:

- What information and data are needed to better understand the community you serve?
- What opportunities might be missed or what blind spots exist due to lack of diversity?
- How can the museum embrace the inclusion of individuals coming from diverse or traditionally marginalized communities?

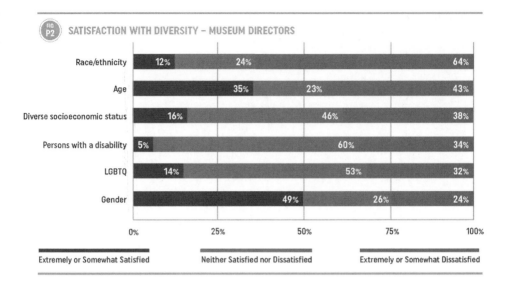

FIG P2 — SATISFACTION WITH DIVERSITY – MUSEUM DIRECTORS

| | Extremely or Somewhat Satisfied | Neither Satisfied nor Dissatisfied | Extremely or Somewhat Dissatisfied |
|---|---|---|---|
| Race/ethnicity | 12% | 24% | 64% |
| Age | 35% | 23% | 43% |
| Diverse socioeconomic status | 16% | 46% | 38% |
| Persons with a disability | 5% | 60% | 34% |
| LGBTQ | 14% | 53% | 32% |
| Gender | 49% | 26% | 24% |

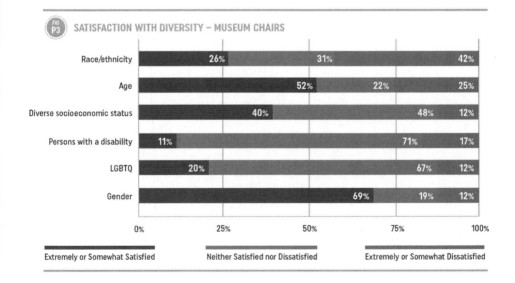

FIG P3 — SATISFACTION WITH DIVERSITY – MUSEUM CHAIRS

| | Extremely or Somewhat Satisfied | Neither Satisfied nor Dissatisfied | Extremely or Somewhat Dissatisfied |
|---|---|---|---|
| Race/ethnicity | 26% | 31% | 42% |
| Age | 52% | 22% | 25% |
| Diverse socioeconomic status | 40% | 48% | 12% |
| Persons with a disability | 11% | 71% | 17% |
| LGBTQ | 20% | 67% | 12% |
| Gender | 69% | 19% | 12% |

## VALUE OF BOARD DIVERSITY AND INCLUSION *percent of "Very Important" rating*

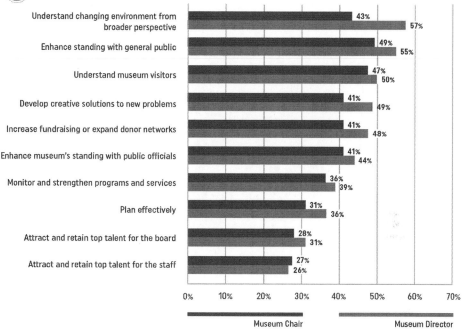

Understand changing environment from broader perspective — 43% / 57%

Enhance standing with general public — 49% / 55%

Understand museum visitors — 47% / 50%

Develop creative solutions to new problems — 41% / 49%

Increase fundraising or expand donor networks — 41% / 48%

Enhance museum's standing with public officials — 41% / 44%

Monitor and strengthen programs and services — 36% / 39%

Plan effectively — 31% / 36%

Attract and retain top talent for the board — 28% / 31%

Attract and retain top talent for the staff — 27% / 26%

0% 10% 20% 30% 40% 50% 60% 70%

Museum Chair — Museum Director

## BOARD ACTIONS RELATED TO DIVERSITY AND INCLUSION

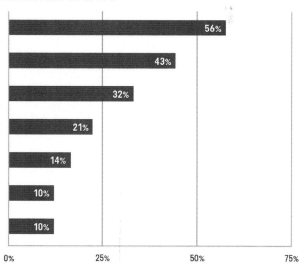

Agreed that it is important to advance the level of board diversity and incorporate diversity into the organization's core values. — 56%

Made explicit and discussed the values and benefits of expanding diversity of the board, and the disadvantages of not doing so. — 43%

Evaluated & modified recruitment efforts specifically to reach potential members from diverse backgrounds. — 32%

Modified organizational policies & procedures to be more inclusive. — 21%

Conducted diversity training for staff and board members. — 14%

Developed a detailed plan of action for the board to become more inclusive, including measures of progress. — 10%

Encouraged resources be allocated to support recruitment of diverse board leaders and to inspire board service. — 10%

0% 25% 50% 75%

# Appendix D

## Selected Resources

- The Andrew W. Mellon Foundation Art Museum Staff Demographic Survey 2015
  https://mellon.org/media/filer_public/ba/99/ba99e53a-48d5-4038-80e1-66f9ba1c020e/awmf_museum_diversity_report_aamd_7-28-15.pdf

- Case Studies in Museum Diversity
  https://mellon.org/resources/news/articles/case-studies-museum-diversity/

- Design for Accessibility: A Cultural Administrators Handbook
  https://www.arts.gov/sites/default/files/Design-for-Accessibility.pdf

- Facing Change: Insights from AAM's DEAI Working Group
  https://www.aam-us.org/programs/diversity-equity-accessibility-and-inclusion/facing-change/

- Family Inclusive Language Chart
  https://incluseum.files.wordpress.com/2014/06/infographic.jpg

- LGBTQ Welcoming Guidelines
  https://www.aam-us.org/wp-content/uploads/2017/11/lgbtq_welcome_guide.pdf

- MASS Action (Museum as Site for Social Action) Readiness Assessment and Tool Kit
  https://www.museumaction.org/resources/

- Museum Board Leadership: A National Report 2017
  https://www.aam-us.org/wp-content/uploads/2018/01/eyizzp-download-the-report.pdf

- National NAGPRA Resources for Museums
  https://www.nps.gov/nagpra/MUSEUMS/INDEX.HTM

- Smithsonian's Guide to Accessible Exhibit Design
  https://www.si.edu/Accessibility/SGAED

- Telling All Our Stories: 10 Steps to Greater DEAI in Museums
  http://cookross.com/wp-content/uploads/2018/05/TellingOurStories-DEAI
  Museums.pdf

- Technical Leaflet 263: What's the Big Idea? Using Listening Sessions to Build
  Relationships and Relevance
  https://learn.aaslh.org/products/technical-leaflet-263-whats-the-big-idea-using
  -listening-sessions-to-build-relationships-and-relevance

# Bibliography

American Alliance of Museums. *Facing Change: Insights from the American Alliance of Museums' Diversity, Equity, Accessibility, and Inclusion Working Group.* Arlington, VA: American Alliance of Museums, 2018.

American Alliance of Museums and Wilkening Consulting. *Museums and Public Opinion 2017.* Arlington, VA: American Alliance of Museums, 2017.

American Library Association. "Public Library Use." Tools, Publications and Resources. Last modified October 2015. Accessed March 23, 2017. http://www.ala.org/tools/libfactsheets/alalibraryfactsheet06.

Association of Art Museum Directors. *Next Practices in Diversity and Inclusion.* New York and Washington, DC: Association of Art Museum Directors, 2016.

Association of Science-Technology Centers and Association of Children's Museums. *2016 Workforce Survey Report.* Washington, DC: Association of Science-Technology Centers, 2016.

Barlow, Clare. *Queer British Art, 1861–1967.* London: Tate Publishing, 2017.

Bennett, Tony. *The Birth of the Museum: History, Theory, Politics, Culture: Policies and Politics.* London and New York: Routledge, 1995.

BoardSource. *Museum Board Leadership 2017: A National Report.* Washington, DC: BoardSource, 2017.

Bohm, David, Donald Factor, and Peter Garett. *Dialogue: A Proposal*, 1991. http://www.david-bohm.net/dialogue/dialogue_proposal.html.

Bourdieu, Pierre. *Distinction: A Social Critique of the Judgement of Taste.* Cambridge, MA: Harvard University Press, 1989.

Bunch, Lonnie. "Flies in the Buttermilk: Museums, Diversity, and the Will to Change." *Museum News*, July/August 2000.

CFED and Institute for Policy Studies. *The Ever-Growing Gap: Without Change, African-American and Latino Families Won't Match White Wealth for Centuries.* Washington, DC: CFED and Institute for Policy Studies, 2016. https://www.ips-dc.org/wp-content/uploads/2016/08/The-Ever-Growing-Gap-CFED_IPS-Final-2.pdf.

Chung, James. *Museums and Society 2034: Trends and Potential Futures.* Center for the Future of Museums Project. Washington, DC: American Association of Museums, 2008.

Cossentino, M., S. Galland, N. Gaud, V. Hilaire, and A. Koukam. "How to Control Emergence of Behaviours in a Holarchy." Paper presented at the Second IEEE International Conference on Self-Adaptive and Self-Organizing Systems Workshops, Isola di San Servolo, Venice, October 20–24, 2008. https://doi.org/10.1109/sasow.2008.28.

Costo, Rupert. "A Statement of Policy." *The Indian Historian* 1, no. 1 (1964): n.p.

Dilenschneider, Colleen. "High Propensity Visitors: The True Attributes of People Attending Museums and Cultural Centers." Know Your Own Bone, October 23, 2013. http://colleen dilen.com/2013/10/23/high-propensity-visitors-the-true-attributes-of-people-attending -museums-and-cultural-centers-data/ (article was removed from website by August 6, 2018).

Farrell, Betty, and Maria Medvedeva. *Demographic Transformation and the Future of Museums.* Center for the Future of Museums Project. Washington, DC: American Association of Museums, 2010.

Foucault, Michel. *The Order of Things: An Archaeology of the Human Sciences.* New York: Vintage Books, 1973.

Gelles, David. "Wooing a New Generation of Museum Patrons." *New York Times.* March 19, 2014. https://www.nytimes.com/2014/03/20/arts/artsspecial/wooing-a-new-generation-of -museum-patrons.html.

General Assembly. *United Nations Declaration on the Rights of Indigenous People.* September 2007, 107th plenary meeting. http://www.un.org/esa/socdev/unpfii/documents/DRIPS_en.pdf.

Gurian, Elaine Heumann. "Intentional Civility." *Curator: The Museum Journal* 57, no. 4 (2014): 473–84. https://doi.org/10.1111/cura.12086.

Habermas, Jürgen. *The Structural Transformation of the Public Sphere: An Inquiry into a Category of Bourgeois Society.* Translated by Thomas Burger with Frederick Lawrence. Cambridge, MA: MIT Press, 1991.

Heaton, James. "Museums and Race." Tronvig Group. Accessed February 26, 2016. http:// www.tronviggroup.com/museums-and-race/.

Incluseum. "Gender Equity and Museums." February 8, 2016. https://incluseum.com/ 2016/02/08/gender-equity-and-museums/.

International Coalition for the Sites of Conscience. *Facilitated Dialogue Training Materials.* 2013 and 2016.

Jennings, Gretchen, and Joanne Jones-Rizzi. "Museums, White Privilege, and Diversity: A Systemic Perspective." *Dimensions*, Special Edition, 2016.

Katz, Philip M., and Elizabeth E. Merritt. *TrendsWatch 2013: Back to the Future.* Center for the Future of Museums Project. Arlington, VA: American Alliance of Museums, 2013. https://www.aam-us.org/wp-content/uploads/2018/04/trendswatch2013.pdf.

Levin, Amy K. (Ed.). *Gender, Sexuality and Museums, A Routledge Reader.* Oxfordshire and New York: Routledge, 2010.

Linzer, Danielle, and Mary Ellen Munley. *Room to Rise: The Lasting Impact of Intensive Teen Programs in Art Museums.* New York: Whitney Museum of American Art, 2015. http:// whitney.org/file_columns/0009/7558/room-to-rise.pdf.

Litwin, Fred. "Not My Rights Movement." *C2C Journal*, December 12, 2016. http://www .c2cjournal.ca/2016/12/not-my-rights-movement/.

Lonetree, Amy. *Decolonizing Museums: Representing Native America in National and Tribal Museums.* Chapel Hill: University of North Carolina Press, 2012.

Lord, Gail Dexter, Ngaire Blankenberg, and Richard L. Florida. *Cities, Museums and Soft Power*. Washington, DC: American Alliance of Museums Press, 2016.

McIntosh, Peggy. "White Privilege: Unpacking the Invisible Knapsack." *Independent School* (Winter 1990).

McKinley, Kelly. "What Is Our Museum's Social Impact? Trying to Understand and Measure How Our Museum Changes Lives in Our Community." Medium, July 10, 2017. https://medium.com/new-faces-new-spaces/what-is-our-museums-social-impact-62525fe88d16.

Miller, Susan. "Native America Writes Back: The Origin of the Indigenous Paradigm in Historiography." *Wicazo Sa Review* 23, no. 2 (2008): 9–28.

Moore, Porchia. "The Danger of the 'D' Word: Museums and Diversity." *Incluseum* (blog), January 20, 2014. http://incluseum.com/2014/01/20/the-danger-of-the-d-word-museums-and-diversity/.

Museum Folkwang. "Konferenzen und Kooperationen." Accessed April 5, 2018. https://www.museum-folkwang.de/de/ueber-uns/forschung/konferenzen-und-kooperationen/konferenzen/queer-exhibitions-queer-curating.html.

MuseumWorkersSpeak. *How Do We Turn the Social Justice Lens Inward? A Conversation about Internal Museum Labor Practices*. AAM 2015 "Rogue Session." N.p.: MuseumWorkersSpeak, 2015. Accessed March 22, 2016. https://drive.google.com/file/d/0B3UU5M-r8dW7M3Jac2d6NmZXcFk/view.

National Endowment for the Arts. *NEA Research Report #57 September 2013*. "How a Nation Engages with Art: Highlights from the 2012 Survey of Public Participation in the Arts." Washington, DC: NEA, 2012. https://www.arts.gov/sites/default/files/highlights-from-2012-sppa-revised-oct-2015.pdf.

Native American Graves Protection and Repatriation Act of 1990, 25 U.S.C. 3001 et seq.

Oakland Museum of California. "Culture + Values." Career Opportunities. www.museumca.org/careers/omca-culture.

Pitman, Bonnie, and Ellen Hirzy. *Excellence and Equity: Education and the Public Dimension of Museums*. Washington, DC: American Association of Museums, 1992.

Queering the Museum Project. "About QTM." Accessed April 5, 2018. https://queeringthemuseum.org/about/.

Reach Advisors. *Museums R+D Research Memo Number 1:8, Museums and Trust*. New York: Reach Advisors, 2015.

Redman, Samuel J. *Bone Rooms*. Cambridge: Harvard University Press, 2016.

Sandell, Richard. "Museums as Agents of Social Inclusion." *Museum Management and Curatorship* 17, no. 4 (1998): 401–18.

Savage, Elinor. "A Call to Action." Arts in a Changing America. Accessed February 19, 2016. http://artsinachangingamerica.org/2016/02/09/a-call-to-action/ (article was removed from website by August 6, 2018).

Schonfeld, Roger, Mariët Westermann, and Liam Sweeney. *The Andrew W. Mellon Foundation: Art Museum Demographic Survey*. New York: The Andrew W. Mellon Foundation, 2015.

Seattle Art Museum. "Careers." About SAM. www.seattleartmuseum.org/about-sam/careers.

Silverman, Lois H. *The Social Work of Museums*. London: Routledge, 2010.

Simon, Harvey. "Black Lives Matter Too." *Huffington Post*, October 19, 2015. http://www.huffingtonpost.com/harvey-simon/black-lives-matter-too_b_8316882.html.

Simon, Nina. *Art of Relevance*. Museum 2.0, 2016.

Sinek, Simon. *Start with Why: How Great Leaders Inspire Everyone to Take Action*. New York: Penguin Press, 2009.

Society for Human Resource Management. "Understanding and Developing Organizational Culture." Toolkits, February 12, 2018. https://www.shrm.org/resourcesandtools/tools-and -samples/toolkits/pages/understandinganddevelopingorganizationalculture.aspx.

Storey, Stephanie. "To Succeed in Business, Major in Art History." *Huffington Post*, December 6, 2017. https://www.huffingtonpost.com/stephanie-storey/to-succeed-in-business-ma_b_ 10117802.html.

Thomas, David A., and Robin J. Ely. "Making Differences Matter: A New Paradigm for Managing Diversity." *Harvard Business Review* (September–October 1996): 70–91.

Trivedi, Nikhil. "Oppression: A Museum Primer." *Incluseum* (blog), February 4, 2015. http:// incluseum.com/2015/02/04/oppression-a-museum-primer/.

Walker, Darren. "Internships Are Not a Privilege." *New York Times*, July 5, 2016. https:// www.nytimes.com/2016/07/05/opinion/breaking-a-cycle-that-allows-privilege-to-go-to -privileged.html.

Wallace Foundation. "YouthALIVE! Program." Accessed March 20, 2016. http://www .wallacefoundation.org/learn-about-wallace/GrantsPrograms/our-initiatives/Past-Initiatives/ Pages/Youth-Alive.aspx (page was removed from website by August 6, 2018).

Weil, Stephen E. *Making Museums Matter*. Washington, DC: Smithsonian Institution, 2002.

Wikipedia. "United States Federal Civil Rights Legislation." Last modified September 17, 2017. https://en.wikipedia.org/wiki/Category:United_States_federal_civil_rights_legislation.

Zickuhr, Kathryn, Lee Rainie, Kristen Purcell, and Maeve Duggan. *How Americans Value Public Libraries in Their Communities. Pew Research Center*. Philadelphia: The Pew Charitable Trusts, 2012.

# Index

153

# About the Editors and Contributors

## JOHNNETTA BETSCH COLE

 Johnnetta Betsch Cole is a principal consultant with Cook Ross. Before assuming her current position, she served for eight years as the director of the Smithsonian National Museum of African Art. After receiving a Ph.D. in anthropology with a specialization in African studies from Northwestern University, Dr. Cole held teaching and administrative positions in anthropology, women's studies, and African American studies at several colleges and universities. She served as the president of both historically Black colleges for women in the United States, Spelman College and Bennett College, a distinction she alone holds. She has authored and edited several books and numerous articles for scholarly and general audiences.

Dr. Cole was the first African American to serve as the chair of the board of the United Way of America. She formerly served on the corporate boards of Home Depot, Merck, and Nation's Bank South and was the first woman to serve on the board of Coca-Cola Enterprises. From 2015 to 2016, she was the president of the Association of Art Museum Directors. Dr. Cole is a senior consulting fellow at the Andrew W. Mellon Foundation. She is a fellow of the American Anthropological Association and a member of the National Academy of Arts and Sciences.

Johnnetta Betsch Cole has received numerous awards and is the recipient of over sixty honorary degrees. Throughout her career and in her published work, speeches, and community service, she consistently addresses issues of race, gender, and other systems of inequality.

## LAURA L. LOTT

Laura L. Lott is president and CEO of the American Alliance of Museums, the only organization representing the entire scope of the museum community. After being named the first woman to lead the organization in 2015, Lott led the development and launch of AAM's strategic plan, which emphasizes topics that alliance members strongly believe are vital to the future viability, relevance, and sustainability of all types and sizes of museums. Strategic focus areas include diversity, equity, accessibility, and inclusion; financial sustainability; and museums' role in P–12 education.

As chief operating officer, Lott led the 2012 relaunch of the alliance, including rebranding the organization and redesigning its membership and excellence programs to be more inclusive, leading to 70 percent membership growth. She is a results-oriented, entrepreneurial, strategic leader with a track record of setting and achieving aggressive programmatic and financial goals. A passionate advocate for strong and engaged boards, Lott frequently speaks to nonprofit and museum boards about governance and strategy.

Prior to joining AAM, Lott worked on the leadership teams of the JASON Project at National Geographic and the MarcoPolo: Internet Content for the Classroom program at the former MCI Foundation. After graduating from American University in Washington, DC, Lott gained public accounting experience at PricewaterhouseCoopers, with a focus on nonprofit clients. Lott is a Virginia-licensed CPA and a private pilot.

## BETH BIENVENU

Dr. Beth Bienvenu is the director of the Office of Accessibility at the National Endowment for the Arts, where she manages the NEA's technical assistance and advocacy work devoted to making the arts accessible for people with disabilities, older adults, veterans, and people in institutional settings. She provides guidance and support to state arts agency staff and professionals working the fields of arts access, creativity and aging, arts and health, universal design, and arts in corrections.

Prior to her work at the NEA, she worked as a policy advisor for the U.S. Department of Labor's Office of Disability Employment Policy (ODEP), and she also served as an adjunct professor for George Mason University's master of arts in arts management program, where she taught courses in arts policy. Dr. Bienvenu has master's degrees in sociology and arts administration from Indiana University and a doctorate in organizational leadership from the University of Oklahoma.

## ANDREA BARNWELL BROWNLEE

Dr. Andrea Barnwell Brownlee is an art historian, curator, writer, and the director of the Spelman College Museum of Fine Art. She has curated and cocurated several exhibitions that have garnered international acclaim. In 2012, Dr. Brownlee and curator Valerie Cassel Oliver of the Virginia Museum of Fine Arts curated the exhibition *Cinema Remixed and Reloaded: Black Women Artists and the Moving Image Since 1970*, and it was the first exhibition assembled by American curators to be presented in the Havana Biennial. She is the author of *Charles White: The David C. Driskell Series of African American Art, Volume I*, as well as several exhibition catalogues. Dr. Brownlee is a widely recognized leader who has garnered praise in areas including curating exhibitions that excavate the contributions of Black women artists, advocating for artists through public art initiatives, and guiding the next generation of curators and museum professionals. She is the recipient of academic, professional, and scholarly awards including the 2013 David C. Driskell Prize in African American Art and Art History from the High Museum of Art and the 2015 James A. Porter Award from Howard University. An alumna of Spelman College, she earned her Ph.D. in art history from Duke University in 2001.

## LONNIE G. BUNCH III

Historian, author, curator, and educator Lonnie G. Bunch III is the founding director of the Smithsonian's National Museum of African American History and Culture. In this position, he advances the museum's mission to tell the American story through the lens of African American history and culture and provides strategic leadership in fundraising, collections, and academic and cultural partnerships. Bunch has spent nearly forty years in the museum field, where he is regarded as one of the nation's leading figures.

A prolific author, he has written on topics ranging from slavery and the black military experience to the

American presidency and the impact of funding and politics on American museums. His books include *Call the Lost Dream Back: Essays on Race, History and Museums* (2010), *Slave Culture: A Documentary Collection of the Slave Narratives* (2014), and *Memories of the Enslaved: Voices from the Slave Narratives* (2015).

Bunch has held teaching positions at George Washington University and American University in Washington, DC, and the University of Massachusetts, Dartmouth. He received undergraduate and graduate degrees from American University in African American and American history. In 2017, he was elected as a member of the American Academy of Arts and Sciences.

## CINNAMON CATLIN-LEGUTKO

Working in museums for more than twenty years, Cinnamon Catlin-Legutko has been a museum director since 2001. Prior to joining the Abbe Museum as president and CEO in 2009, Catlin-Legutko was the director of the General Lew Wallace Study and Museum where she led the organization to the National Medal for Museum Service in 2008. She is currently a board member of Maine Humanities Council and the American Alliance of Museums. She is the coeditor and chapter author for the Small Museum Toolkit, a six-book series that was published in 2012. Her most recent publication, *Museum Administration 2.0*, was published in 2016.

## EDUARDO DÍAZ

Eduardo Díaz, director of the Smithsonian Latino Center, is a thirty-five-year veteran of the Latino cultural field. The center supports research, exhibitions, public and educational programs, digital content, collections, and publications about the Latino experience in the United States. Díaz is the former executive director of the National Hispanic Cultural Center in Albuquerque and served as San Antonio's director of cultural affairs. Díaz has a law degree from University of California, Davis, and a bachelor's in Latin American studies from San Diego State University.

# WILLIAM UNDERWOOD EILAND

A native of Sprott, Alabama, William Underwood Eiland is the director of the Georgia Museum of Art at the University of Georgia. He has a bachelor's degree from Birmingham-Southern College and master's and doctoral degrees from the University of Virginia. Eiland has edited and contributed to more than sixty publications. He has served on the boards of the American Alliance of Museums, the Southeastern Museums Conference, and the Georgia Association of Museums and Galleries; was a trustee of the Association of Art Museum Directors; and was chairman of the Arts and Artifacts Indemnity Advisory Panel for the National Endowment for the Arts. Since 2013, he has been a trustee of the International Council of Museums. He served as vice chairman of AAM's Accreditation Commission. Among his many honors, in 2013, Eiland received the American Alliance of Museums Distinguished Service Award in recognition of his contributions to the field on a national level. Most recently, in October 2017, he received a Governor's Award for the Arts and Humanities for his service to Georgia.

# KAYWIN FELDMAN

Kaywin Feldman has been the Nivin and Duncan MacMillan Director and President of the Minneapolis Institute of Art (Mia) since 2008. Feldman oversees the museum's staff of 250, its fine art collection of over 89,000 objects, its 473,000-square-foot facility, and an annual operating budget of $32 million. During Feldman's tenure, Mia has strengthened its national presence with ambitious special exhibitions; championed the use of digital technologies to support and enhance audience engagement; and strategically acquired major works of art for its permanent collection. Feldman serves on the boards of National Arts Strategies (NAS) and the Chipstone Foundation. She is also a member of the Bizot Group. She is a past president of the Association of Art Museum Directors (AAMD) and a former chair of the American Alliance of Museums (AAM). Feldman received an honorary doctor of fine arts degree from the Memphis College of Art in 2008 and holds an M.A. in art history from the Courtauld Institute of Art at the University of London and an M.A. from the Institute of Archaeology at the University of London. Her specialties are Dutch and Flemish art and Greek and Roman archaeology.

## HABEN GIRMA

As the first Deafblind person to graduate from Harvard Law School, Haben Girma advocates for equal opportunities for people with disabilities. President Obama named her a White House Champion of Change. She received the Helen Keller Achievement Award and a spot on Forbes 30 Under 30. Girma travels the world consulting and public speaking, teaching clients the benefits of fully accessible products and services. She's a talented storyteller who helps people frame difference as an asset. She resisted society's low expectations, choosing to create her own pioneering story. Girma is working on a book that will be published by Hachette in 2019.

## ELAINE HEUMANN GURIAN

Elaine Heumann Gurian is a consultant/advisor to museums and visitor centers that rebuild or reinvent themselves. She grew up in Queens, New York, was an elementary school art teacher, and to her surprise, began her unplanned museum career in 1969 in a mobile crafts unit in Boston after the death of Martin Luther King. Since that time, she has served as senior staff to museums interested in visitor focus and inclusion, as a deputy assistant secretary at the Smithsonian Institution, and since 1993, as the senior consultant to many national and memorial museums under construction around the world. Gurian serves as a visiting faculty member to many museum graduate programs and middle management training institutes. Gurian thrives in association politics, holding many elected positions. Her writings are widely published and included in many academic courses. www.egurian.com.

## NATANYA KHASHAN

Natanya Khashan serves as the subject matter expert on diversity and inclusion in museums and as the marketing and events specialist at Cook Ross, a consulting firm

specializing in diversity and inclusion. Khashan has previously served as the marketing and communications manager of Montgomery County, Maryland's largest visual arts center, spearheading efforts to create more inclusive gallery spaces and establish arts education after-school initiatives for immigrant families. Prior to reclaiming her hometown of Washington, DC, she served as a curatorial fellow at the Massachusetts College of Art and Design Bakalar and Paine Galleries and taught at the Institute of Contemporary Art, Boston. Khashan has authored and coauthored publications on developing socially inclusive museums, including a thought paper coauthored with Johnnetta B. Cole, *The Museum IDEA: Addressing Inclusion, Diversity, Equity, and Accessibility in American Museums*. Khashan has a master's in arts management and certification in technology in arts management from American University and a bachelor of fine arts degree from Massachusetts College of Art and Design.

## LISA SASAKI

Lisa Sasaki is the director of the Smithsonian Asian Pacific American Center (APAC), a museum without walls that brings Asian Pacific American history, art, and culture to communities through innovative museum experiences online and throughout the United States. Previously she was the director of the Audience and Civic Engagement Center at the Oakland Museum of California and the director of program development at the Japanese American National Museum in Los Angeles. Sasaki has served as president of the Western Museums Association's board of directors, as a member of the American Alliance of Museums' diversity equity access and inclusion working group, and as an advisor on the advisory council for the Council of Jewish American Museums. She is a frequent guest lecturer for museum studies graduate programs and has also lectured internationally for organizations like ICOM-China and the Museums and Galleries of Queensland in Australia.

## CECILE SHELLMAN

Cecile Shellman is a museum consultant who most recently served as the diversity catalyst for Carnegie Museums of Pittsburgh. In that role she responds to initiatives relevant to diversity, inclusion, and accessibility at Carnegie Museum of Art, Carnegie Museum of Natural History, Carnegie Science Center, and the Andy Warhol Museum. Past appointments include director for visual arts and exhibitions at the August Wilson Center; program manager for Pittsburgh Public Schools' Culturally Responsive Arts Education initiative; education coordinator at the John F. Kennedy Presidential Library and Museum in Boston; director of education at Heckscher Museum of Art, New York; and education curator at the Museum of Church History and Art, Salt Lake City. She serves on the Associated Artists of Pittsburgh board of directors, Sports and Exhibitions Authority art committee, cochair of the American Alliance of Museums' DIVCOM professional committee, and AAM national planning committee. Shellman holds a BFA in painting from Brigham Young University and a CMS from Harvard University. She enjoys spending time with her husband, Spencer, and is a fiercely competitive Scrabble player.

## CARLOS TORTOLERO

Carlos Tortolero is the founder and president of the National Museum of Mexican Art (NMMA), the first Latino museum accredited by the American Alliance of Museums. Since opening in 1987, the museum has become a national model for its exhibits, performances, arts education programs, and advocacy on cultural equity issues. NMMA contains over ten thousand objects in its permanent collection. The museum is the only organization to have won two White House national awards for excellence in youth arts programming. NMMA also has an extensive performing arts program. Twenty exhibitions organized by the NMMA have traveled across the country, and eight have traveled to Mexico.

From 1975 to 1987, Tortolero worked as a teacher, counselor, and administrator in the Chicago public school system. He has served on numerous boards, including those of the University of Illinois, American Alliance of Museums, Chicago Department of Cultural Affairs, Smithsonian Latino Center, and the Illinois Humanities Council. He is a recipient of an honorary degree from Columbia College (Chicago) and an honorary degree from the University of Illinois (Chicago). Tortolero is the coauthor of *Mexican Chicago* and has written articles for national and international publications. He has also taught classes at University of Illinois at Chicago, the School of the Art Institute, and Northwestern University. Tortolero has a B.A. in secondary education and history from the University of Illinois at Chicago and an M.A. in bilingual education supervision from Chicago State University.

He has presented throughout the United States and Mexico and has also spoken at conferences in France, Sweden, and Argentina. He has won numerous awards for his work, including the Ohtli Award, which is the highest honor given by Mexico to individuals "Who have distinguished themselves in the services of the Mexican community outside of Mexico." He was named by the *Chicago Sun-Times* as one of the two hundred most prominent Illinoisans in two hundred years of history and was awarded the City of Chicago's highest honor in the arts—the Fifth Star Award. He also received the Chicago History Museum "Making History" Award.

## DARREN WALKER

Darren Walker is president of the Ford Foundation, an international social justice philanthropy with a $13 billion endowment and $600 million in annual grant making. For two decades, he has been a leader in the nonprofit and philanthropic sectors. Walker led the philanthropy committee that helped bring a resolution to the city of Detroit's historic bankruptcy and chairs the U.S. Alliance on Impact Investing. He cochairs New York City's Commission on City Art, Monuments, and Markers and serves on the Commission on the Future of Rikers Island Correctional Institution and the UN International Labor Organization Commission on the Future of Work. He also serves on the boards of Carnegie Hall, the High Line, and the Committee to Protect Journalists and is a member of the Council on Foreign Relations and the American Academy of Arts and Sciences.

## W. RICHARD WEST JR.

W. Richard West Jr. serves as the president and CEO of the Autry Museum of the American West in Los Angeles and is director emeritus and founding director

of the Smithsonian Institution's National Museum of the American Indian. He is a citizen of the Cheyenne and Arapaho Nation of Oklahoma and a member of the Southern Cheyenne Society of Peace Chiefs. West currently is a member of the board of directors of ICOM-US and the International Coalition of Sites of Conscience and previously served on the boards of the Ford Foundation, Stanford University, and the Kaiser Family Foundation. He also was chair of the board of directors of the American Alliance of Museums (1998–2000) and vice president of the International Council of Museums (2007–2010).